Brave Lives

Brave Lives

The Members and Staff of The Travellers Club
who fell in the Great War

Pen & Sword
MILITARY

First published in Great Britain in 2016 by
Pen & Sword Military
an imprint of
Pen & Sword Books Ltd
47 Church Street
Barnsley
South Yorkshire
S70 2AS

ISBN 978 1 47389 584 3

A CIP catalogue record for this book is available from the British
Library

Typeset in Ehrhardt by
Mac Style Ltd, Bridlington, East Yorkshire
Printed and bound in the UK by CPI Group (UK) Ltd,
Croydon, CR0 4YY

Pen & Sword Books Ltd incorporates the imprints of Pen & Sword
Archaeology, Atlas, Aviation, Battleground, Discovery, Family
History, History, Maritime, Military, Naval, Politics, Railways,
Select, Transport, True Crime, and Fiction, Frontline Books, Leo
Cooper, Praetorian Press, Seaforth Publishing and Wharncliffe.

For a complete list of Pen & Sword titles please contact
PEN & SWORD BOOKS LIMITED
47 Church Street, Barnsley, South Yorkshire, S70 2AS, England
E-mail: enquiries@pen-and-sword.co.uk
Website: www.pen-and-sword.co.uk

Contents

Foreword

Field Marshal The Lord Bramall, KG, GCB, OBE, MC

Much has been written and much more will be written to commemorate the Great War and those who died and suffered in it. Individuals and institutions bring their own perspectives to the themes of conflict, bravery and loss. At The Travellers Club ever since 1920 we have been constantly reminded of the 50 members and staff who died in service during the Great War by the memorial outside the Coffee Room. The names, ranks, decorations and service details of the fallen are cut into a piece of marble three metres high by two metres wide. No-one can miss it. That was the point of putting it there. I have often stood before it and reflected on the individuals, some of whose names were familiar and others unknown to me. On the way to or from the Coffee Room my guests have on many occasions asked me, perhaps because I was a soldier, about the Fifty. It gives me great pleasure, therefore, to commend to you *Brave Lives: the Members and Staff of The Travellers Club who fell in the Great War*. The purpose of this book is to go beyond the names and ranks and decorations and tell us more about these men, their backgrounds, the main events of their lives, their interests and the circumstances of their deaths. It has been a team effort with members of the club and some relations 'adopting a warrior' and, under the guidance of an expert

Editorial Board, researching and writing up their lives. I hope that you enjoy reading it and consider it to be a fitting commemoration of these men whom, but for their deaths in the war, some of us would have met and known at The Travellers Club.

Preface

In August 2014 a notice appeared in the club newsletter under the heading 'Adopt a Warrior'. The notice announced the intention to produce a book that would remember in an appropriate way the 50 members and staff who died in service during the Great War. It asked for volunteers to research the lives of the Fifty. There was an enthusiastic response from members and, as the word got out, from descendants of the Fifty who were not members of the club.

The original suggestion for the book and its title came from Sheila Markham, the Librarian, who has worked tirelessly in every step of its production. The idea was then taken forward and brought to life by Jeremy Taylor, the Chairman of the Library Committee at the time. David Broadhead, the Secretary, has accompanied our efforts in the same able and unobtrusive way in which he plays the piano.

In the autumn of 2014 an Editorial Board was formed. We were fortunate to secure the services of Michael Burleigh, Christopher Coker, Alan Guy and David Twiston Davies, whose expert guidance has supported this project throughout.

The Editorial Board reviewed the biographical forms that each researcher had filled out. Biographical notes for each of the Fifty have been produced from these forms. Not surprisingly the amount of information that was available varied from individual to individual and interesting or unusual facts were known about some and not others. After much discussion, the Editorial Board asked for profiles in the personal style of each researcher to be written of 29 of the Fifty. It was their belief that the objective of the book would best be served by producing a work that held the interest of the reader and that scant details and unconnected facts would not achieve that end. This project is motivated by respect and gratitude for *all* of the Fifty and we recognize the unique sacrifice of each.

From the beginning Lord Bramall has been this project's patron. He has met the researchers and offered continual encouragement. John Martin Robinson, the club's historian, has kindly given us a taste of his forthcoming book by writing about The Travellers Club in 1914.

The biographical notes are in alphabetical order and the profiles are in the order of date of death.

I should like to thank Henry Wilson, Matthew Jones, Jon Wilkinson and Mat Blurton from Pen & Sword for their skill and patience, and Christopher Phipps, our indexer, for helping us to navigate so many names and places.

Finally, I should like to thank the army of volunteers who have cheerfully and energetically supported the production of this book over the last two years: Charles Abel Smith, Christopher Arnander, Hugh Boscawen, Robert Boyle, Nicholas Brainsby, Lord Bramall, Griselda Brook, Edward Buchan, Michael Burleigh, Paul Burnand, Richard Carden, Subhash Chandran, Christopher Coker, Andrew Cormack, Nigel Cox, Piers Craven, David Crichton, Justin Davies, Judy Dyer,

Paul Dyer, Joanna Fitzalan Howard, Alan Guy, William Hanbury-Tenison, Jane Horner, Daniel Hunt, Christopher Jones, Olivia Jones, Jennifer King, Bill Knight, Cherry Ann Knott, Anthony Layden, Richard Legge, Jonathan Lindley, Edward Lucas, Alec McCluskey, Simon Murray, Richard Nunneley, Algernon Percy, James Pettit, Clive Porter, Trevor Purnell, John Martin Robinson, Nicholas Roskill, David Smurthwaite, Justin Staples, Jeremy Taylor, Robert Taylor, David Twiston Davies, Philip Vallance, John Wates, Roger Westbrook, David White, Paul Winby and Francis Witts.

Julian Tunnicliffe

The Travellers Club in 1914

When the tragedy of the Great War overwhelmed The Travellers Club, it was approaching its centenary and had established itself since its foundation in 1819 as one of the most successful and socially exclusive clubs, if not the most socially exclusive club, in London. An article in a series on leading London clubs published in the *Illustrated London News* in 1898 had described it as 'full of cabinet ministers and dukes' but that all were 'treated alike within its portals'. This was attributed not to any egalitarian sense but the fact that all the 'members were of such distinction'. When war broke out, the ex-cabinet ministers included A.J. Balfour, former Prime Minister, and the Marquess of Lansdowne, former Foreign Secretary who had negotiated the Entente Cordiale. The then Foreign Secretary, Sir Edward Grey, was also a member.

The dukes among the membership in the late-Victorian and Edwardian period numbered five Royal Dukes – York, Connaught, Cambridge, Teck and Saxe-Coburg – and 18 others including Norfolk, Wellington, Sutherland, Richmond, Northumberland, Leeds, Westminster, Somerset and Buccleuch, many of them depicted in the club's collection of 186 *Vanity Fair* cartoons of Victorian members. The Travellers had more dukes in the late-Victorian and Edwardian periods than any other London club, including White's. The club's trustees were men of great distinction and all were Knights of the Garter, the Duke of Abercorn, the Marquess of Lansdowne, the Marquess of Bath, the Earl of Derby, and Earl Cadogan. Even the club Secretary was titled. Colonel Frank Carandini was Marquis Sarzano, an ex-army officer born in India. He was of Italian descent, a noble of Modena, and a member of the same family as Cardinal Consalvi, the Vatican representative at the Congress of Vienna in 1814–15 who had been a friend of Lord Castlereagh, the club's founder. His grandson, the actor Christopher Lee, was famous as Dracula. The Marquis Sarzano had been granted a Royal Licence to use his foreign title in England, which had involved changing his name on the club's cheques, bank account and other official documents. He remained the Secretary until 1916.

The membership in general included many of the fourth or fifth generation of the club's founding families: Fremantle, Antrobus, Legh, Kerr, Leveson Gower, Cavendish, Cust, Cockerell, Hope, FitzRoy. Sir Almeric FitzRoy, Secretary of the Privy Council, was Chairman of the Library Committee in 1914 and was to become the club's Chairman for the third time during the war, from 1916 to 1919. In 1915 he suggested that a 'Roll of Honour' containing the names of those who died in the war should be posted in the Morning Room.

The close tie-up with the Foreign Office and the world of diplomacy existed in 1914 but was not as dominant as it became after the Great War and in the middle of the twentieth century; it included figures like Lord Carnock and his younger son Harold Nicolson. The latter was responsible as a junior official at the Foreign Office for serving the correct form of the Declaration of War on the German Ambassador Prince Lichnowsky at the Imperial German Embassy in Carlton

Gardens where the inhabitants could be clearly seen from the windows of The Travellers' Library. Nicolson was very embarrassed by this task, as the ambassador, who was a strong anglophile and had done everything he could to stop the two countries drifting into war, was an honorary member of the club as a senior foreign diplomat. He thought that Nicolson had come to say a personal goodbye on the eve of the ambassador's departure from London and was moved by the young man's kindness, a misunderstanding which pained the bearer in the bellicose circumstances.

The great majority of the members in the late-Victorian age and up to the outbreak of war were traditional landowners including many of the greatest in England or their heirs. Apart from the dukes and trustees, they numbered men like the Marquess of Clanricarde, the Earl of Ancaster, the Earl of Airlie, the Earl of Durham, the Earl of Pembroke, the Marquess of Bute, Lord Lovat and Lord Leconfield, who between them owned millions of acres and many of the greatest historic houses in Britain. It was this class, with its patriotic sense of aristocratic military duty, which was especially badly affected by the war and its aftermath, with the concomitant increase in taxes and death duties. It is no coincidence that the Great War memorials at White's and The Travellers have the longest lists of casualties of the non-military West End clubs.

From its foundation The Travellers had had a certain proportion of naval and military officers from the Duke of Wellington and Marquess of Anglesey downwards; service in the Peninsular War, Egypt, and France providing the necessary travel qualification of 500 miles from London. This military contingent had continued. During the

Crimean War all three of the generals, the Earl of Cardigan, the Earl of Lucan and Lord Raglan, and the Commander of the Mediterranean Fleet, Admiral Lord Lyons, were all members of the club, as was the winner of one of the first VCs, the future Lord Wantage. In the late nineteenth century, the services were the preferred occupation for younger sons in aristocratic families. The denizens of smart regiments, therefore, continued to be well represented in the club in the years leading up to the war. The Travellers proved a regular winner of Lord Cheylesmore's Shield for rifle shooting in inter-club competitions in the early twentieth century; and not just the members, the staff also put in a good performance, the Hall page boy, Owen Jones, winning the junior shield with Silver Medal for Boys in 1910. The Committee sent him the club's enthusiastic congratulations.

In the early twentieth century, the club maintained its strong historic connection with travel and the more professional bodies which had spun off from it in the Victorian period such as the Raleigh Club, the Alpine Club and the Royal Geographical Society. The President of the latter was ex-officio an honorary member of The Travellers from the 1890s onwards. Some of the most colourful late-Victorian and Edwardian 'explorers in Byronic mould' were members including Wilfrid Scawen Blunt who spent much of his life in the Levant and Egypt, Aubrey Herbert who invented modern Albania, John Buchan, and not least Sir Francis Younghusband of Tibetan fame and the first Englishman to visit Lhasa. He dreamt up the idea of a crusading 'Travellers Battalion', formed of explorers, adventurers and mountaineers, at the outbreak of war but this was stamped on by the War Office which by that stage considered him to be a quixotic liability and too old. Instead of adventurous derring-do, Sir Francis spent the war years on the Library Committee and supervising the club's newspapers.

In 1914 the club building was in splendid condition much as Barry had designed and built it in 1828–32 but modernised with electric light, Otis lift and a telephone. It had been looked after by Barry's son Charles Barry, junior, in the late nineteenth century and latterly by John Macvicar Anderson the relation and successor of William Burn, the leading mid-Victorian country house architect. Macvicar Anderson was the consultant architect to five leading St James's clubs including Brooks's. He was responsible for a major re-arrangement of The Travellers in 1910–11 when the Coffee Room was moved upstairs to the original drawing rooms on the Pall Mall frontage, and the former Coffee Room, over-looking the garden on the ground floor, was converted to the Smoking Room. At the same time the arcaded alcove off the Inner Hall was tactfully formed by an extension into the courtyard, also by Macvicar Anderson. Both these changes were designed to provide space for smoking on the main floor, the demand for which had been growing since the Crimean War, and to which the opposition of some of the members had finally been overcome in the Edwardian period. By the Great War, smoking was allowed in all the club rooms, and on the staircase, but never in the Library.

The staff of the club, amounting to over 30, had been remarkably stable and long-serving in the late-Victorian and Edwardian period. It was run on socially responsible, even paternalistic, lines with annual summer holidays, and a Staff Benevolent Fund to provide pensions, before these were made compulsory by Lloyd George in 1910. They had their own roast joint of meat in the Servants Hall every day, and more meals were served to the staff than to the members. The club had discontinued its pew in a local Chapel of Ease for lack of use in the 1880s, but the club provided a doctor and treatment in Charing Cross Hospital specially for the staff, and compulsory inoculation was a condition of service. All the staff lived in before the war, two thirds being unmarried; with bedrooms for the maids in the attic over the Library, and dormitories for the men in the garden mezzanine and the basement on that side. In the early 1900s the staff was British, a foreign language-speaking waiter, which had been a requirement in 1819, no longer being necessary. The exception was the cook who was always French. Despite this he was always called the cook, the name chef only being adopted in the 1890s. A new French chef Alcide Mâne had been appointed in summer 1914. His sudden departure was the first sign of the impact of war in August 1914 when he was called up to the French Colours. Against all the odds he returned unscathed in 1918. Otherwise the club, and especially its membership, was changed forever by the Great War. The tragic list of names on the War Memorial illustrates the world which was lost.

John Martin Robinson

The War Memorial

The War Memorial was completed in 1920. There are some oddities about it, perhaps most notably that the letter cutter did not put the names in precise alphabetical order. The sequence of first letters of surnames is correct but, for example, Brabazon comes before Boscawen and Stucley before Sandeman. Some of the surnames are in a form that differed from the family's own usage, for example, Kennett instead of Barrington-Kennett and Makgill-Crichton instead of Maitland Makgill Crichton, probably because of limited space. The only visible correction is in the case of Ryder, whose brother, the Earl of Harrowby, noted an incorrect second initial on a visit to the club and asked for it to be corrected.

Of the Fifty, 48 were members and two were staff. In 1914 there were about 800 members of the club. The 48 therefore represented about 6 per cent of the membership, though of course a much higher proportion of those who were capable of military service.

The services are unevenly represented: 40 (or 80 per cent) were in the Army, five in the Navy and four in what was then the Royal Flying Corps. In fact Viscount Ipswich died in pilot training in April 1918, just 23 days after the Royal Air Force had been formed out of the merger of the Royal Flying Corps and the Royal Naval Air Service. Charles Bruce was not a combatant at all. He volunteered to help in any way he could and became a Commandant of a Field Hospital in Belgium. There after only five weeks he contracted enteric fever. He died in October 1915 aged 50.

As John Martin Robinson has explained, in the last two decades of the nineteenth and first decade of the twentieth century the club was very socially exclusive. There is ample evidence for this in the old candidates' books. Page after page is crossed through: the applicant withdrawing at his or his proposer's request. One of the 48, Samuel Cockerell, a descendant of the supplier of the cast of the Bassae frieze in the Library, was elected on the fourth time of trying. It generally took three or four years between a candidate's name going in the book and being elected, if he was elected at all. It is a further reflection of this social exclusivity that 28 of the 48 (or 58 per cent) went to Eton. No other school accounted for more than two. There were three from Catholic schools: Beaumont, Downside and Stonyhurst.

Another notable fact was how military the club was. Of the 48, 30 (or 63 per cent) were or had been in military service before the war. The professions were sparsely represented – four barristers, three merchant bankers – and practically no-one in trade. Amongst the merchant bankers were Valentine Fleming of Robert Fleming & Co., whom we have to thank for his son, Ian Fleming, Eustace Gibbs of Antony Gibbs & Sons and Patrick Shaw Stewart of Baring Brothers. George Sandeman had a foot in two camps: he was a barrister and wine merchant and shipper – on the port side.

Given how many of the 48 had military careers it is not surprising that 11 went to Sandhurst or Woolwich. 23 (or 48 per cent) went to university: 16 to Oxford and seven to Cambridge, though Trinity, Cambridge accounted for six, the highest number of any college.

The average age of the Fifty at death was 36. The oldest to die was Charles Pretor-Pinney, a career soldier, who died in April 1917 at the Battle of Arras six weeks before his 53rd birthday. Next oldest was Rear Admiral Sir Robert Arbuthnot who died at sea at the Battle of Jutland in May 1916 at 52. The youngest to die was Kenneth Mackenzie who was 24 and a quarter when he was killed on the Hohenzollern Redoubt at the Battle of Loos in September 1915. He had been 'balloted for and elected' on 10 February of the same year. He had been a member for just seven months. We know he landed at Boulogne in May: it is possible that he never visited the club after his election.

The deaths of the Fifty were weighted heavily to the earlier years of the war: 10 in 1914, 21 in 1915, 7 in 1916, 8 in 1917 and 4 in 1918. The first to be killed was Gerald Ponsonby on 31 August 1914, just under four weeks since the beginning of the war, during the British Expeditionary Force's withdrawal from Mons. The final death was William Leveson Gower who was killed by a shell on 9 October 1918 in the Battle of Cambrai, just over four weeks before the war was to end. The deaths of any members and staff after 11 November 1918 as a result of injuries sustained in the war are not recorded on the memorial.

Finally, we come to the two members of staff. We know very little about Ernest Chittenden. He was born at Wellington Barracks, his father being Colour Sergeant, 2nd Battalion, Scots Guards. Ernest was the Head Waiter. He enlisted in October 1914, married Florence Chambers, a waitress but not at the club, in September 1915 and went missing in action at the age of 34 on 29 April 1917. It appears that Florence was the sister of the Head Waiter before Ernest. Florence did not remarry and lived in the marital home, 90 Honeywell Road, Wandsworth, until she died in November 1956 at the age of 69. The memorial describes him as Sergeant Chittenden, though army records show him to have been a Corporal.

Frederick Corley, whose middle initial was C and not E as on the memorial, was also a waiter. He was born the son of a blacksmith and wheelwright in Caston, Norfolk, 15 miles from Euston Hall, the home of Viscount Ipswich. He worked in service at Denstone College, joined the Royal Norfolk Regiment at 18 but then in December 1912, at 25, returned to civilian life and employment with the club, while remaining in the army reserves. He was mobilised on 16 August 1914. He was promoted several times and recognized as being of officer material. He was commissioned on 24 December 1916. He was wounded twice in action and married a nurse whom he had met in hospital in February 1917. He was killed on 12 April 1918 at the age of 30, five weeks before his son was born.

Julian Tunnicliffe

Biographical Notes

Key to biographical notes

SURNAME, given names, decorations and honours.* Date of birth – date of death. Father's name and mother's maiden name. Wife's maiden name. Education. Signature of proposer and date elected (some signatures are illegible and some pages of the candidates' books have been damaged by water). Occupation. Rank and service or regiment at time of death. Circumstances of death. Place where buried or commemorated.

ABEL SMITH, Wilfrid Robert, CMG.* 13 September 1870– 19 May 1915. Robert Abel Smith and the Hon. Isabel Adeane. Violet Somerset. Eton and Sandhurst. C.W. Fremantle, 20 February 1900. Soldier. Lieutenant-Colonel, 2nd Battalion, Grenadier Guards. Died of wounds at Festubert. Buried Le Touret Military Cemetery (Plot II, Row D, Grave 14).

ARBUTHNOT, Sir Robert Keith, Bt, KCB, MVO.* 23 March 1864– 31 May 1916. Sir William Arbuthnot, Bt, and Alice Thompson. Lina Macleay. HMS *Britannia*. Chas. Hotham, 25 February 1903. Sailor. Rear Admiral flying his flag in HMS *Defence*, leading 1st Cruiser Squadron. Died at sea in the Battle of Jutland. No known grave: Plymouth Naval Memorial (Panel 10).

---

* See profile

BARRINGTON-KENNETT, Victor Annesley.* 16 June 1887–
13 March 1916. Lieutenant-Colonel Brackley Barrington-Kennett
and Ellinor Austen. Unmarried. Eton, Sandhurst and Balliol College,
Oxford. H.A. Lascelles, [proposed 19 June 1913]. Soldier. Major and
Squadron Commander, 4th Squadron, Royal Flying Corps. Shot down
by Max Immelmann while flying a Bristol Scout near Serre. Buried
Miraumont Communal Cemetery (A1).

BOSCAWEN, The Hon. George Edward, DSO.* 6 December 1888–
7 June 1918. Evelyn Boscawen, 7th Viscount Falmouth, and Kathleen
Douglas-Pennant. Unmarried. Eton and the Royal Military Academy,
Woolwich. V. Dawson, 2 March 1910. Soldier. Brevet Major, Royal
Field Artillery. Died of wounds in a German hospital at Notre-Dame
de Liesse, near Laon. Buried originally in Notre-Dame de Liesse
German Military Cemetery, but his grave was lost. La Ville-aux-Bois
British Cemetery.

BRABAZON, The Hon. Ernest William Maitland Molyneux, DSO.*
22 March 1884–17 June 1915. Reginald Brabazon, 12th Earl of Meath,
and Mary Maitland. Dorothy Ricardo. Dover College and Sandhurst.
Meath, 19 February 1900. Soldier. Captain, Coldstream Guards.
Killed by a shell while inspecting a machine-gun post near Givenchy.
Buried Cambrin Churchyard Extension (E 37).

BRIDGEMAN, The Hon. Richard Orlando Beaconsfield, DSO.
28 February 1879–9 January 1917. George Bridgeman, 4th Earl of
Bradford, and Frances Lumley. Unmarried. Nothing known of his
education. Buccleuch, 12 February 1908. Sailor. Commander of HMS
Hyacinth. Drowned in the Rufiji river, Tanzania, on active service

following mechanical failure of a sea-plane while on a reconnaissance mission. Buried Dar es Salaam War Cemetery (Plot I, Row A, Grave 6).

BRUCE, Charles Thomas. 21 February 1865–23 October 1915. The Hon. Thomas Bruce and Sarah Thornhill. First, Gwendolen Speir, then Edith Parker. Westminster and Magdalene College, Cambridge. [Illegible], 9 March 1894. Private means. Commandant of a Field Hospital in Belgium. Died of enteric fever contracted while on duty in Flanders. Buried St Margaret's Churchyard, Rottingdean, East Sussex.

CAMPBELL, Allan William George. 20 October 1884–20 September 1914. Allan Campbell and Diamantina 'Nina' Bowen. Lady Moya Browne. Eton and New College, Oxford. Charles S. Scott, 20 February 1906. Soldier, then in June 1914 adopted as Unionist parliamentary candidate for Doncaster. Lieutenant attached to the 1st Battalion, Coldstream Guards. Killed in enemy bombardment in the First Battle of the Aisne on the Chemin des Dames at Vendresse-et-Troyon. Buried Vendresse British Cemetery (Plot III, Row J, Grave 9).

CAVENDISH, Lord John Spencer, DSO.* 25 March 1875–20 October 1914. Lord Edward Cavendish and the Hon. Emma Lascelles. Unmarried. Eton and Trinity College, Cambridge. Arthur Butler, 27 February 1899. Soldier. Major, the 1st Life Guards. Killed by Maxim-gun fire while walking forward to his squadron's advanced troop on a ridge outside Messines. Buried Cabaret-Rouge British Cemetery, Souchez (Plot XXI, Row C, Grave 26).

CHITTENDEN, Ernest Sydney. 23 October 1882–29 April 1917. Richard Chittenden and Emily Watkins. Florence Chambers. Nothing

14   Brave Lives

known of his education. Head Waiter at The Travellers Club. Corporal, 22nd Battalion, Royal Fusiliers. Missing in action. No known grave: Arras Memorial (Bay 3).

COCKERELL, Samuel Pepys. 12 May 1880–20 March 1915. William Cockerell and Sidney Davies. Unmarried. Eton and Trinity College, Cambridge. C.W. Fremantle, 18 February 1914. Foreign Office. 2nd Lieutenant, Royal Flying Corps, Military Wing. Died of smallpox in Ismailia, Egypt. Buried Ismailia War Memorial Cemetery (A 117).

COKE, Langton Sacheverell. 25 January 1878–31 October 1914. Colonel William Coke and Caroline Heugh. Dorothy Huntingford. Educated in France and Germany. M. FitzGerald, 9 February 1911. Soldier, then civil servant. Lieutenant, 1st Battalion, Irish Guards. Killed at Klein Zillebeke in the First Battle of Ypres. Buried originally in the garden of a farm at Klein Zillebeke which was obliterated in subsequent action. No known grave: Menin Gate (Panel 11).

CORLEY, Frederick Charles.* 15 November 1887–12 April 1918. Charles Corley and Rebecca Chapman. Margaret Morrison. Nothing known of his education. Waiter at The Travellers Club, formerly a soldier. 2nd Lieutenant, 8th Battalion Border Regiment. Killed at Kortepyp near Neuve-Eglise. No known grave: Ploegsteert Memorial (Panel 6).

CUNLIFFE, Sir Foster Hugh Egerton, Bt.* 17 August 1875–10 July 1916. Sir Robert Cunliffe, Bt, and Eleanor Leigh. Unmarried. Eton and New College, Oxford. [Illegible], 21 February 1900. Military historian. Fellow and latterly Estates Bursar of All Souls College, Oxford. Major, 13th Battalion, the Rifle Brigade. Died of wounds at

Ovillers la Boiselle in the Battle of the Somme. Buried Bapaume Post Military Cemetery (Plot I, Row G, Grave 3).

DASENT, Manuel.* 13 May 1879–5 June 1916. Sir John Dasent and Ellen Codrington. Unmarried. HMS *Britannia*. C.G. Barrington, 20 February 1901. Royal Navy. Commander of HMS *Hampshire*. Died when *Hampshire* was sunk by a mine. No known grave: Lyness Royal Naval Cemetery (F 12A).

DAWSON, Richard Long. 23 June 1879–20 November 1914. The Hon. Richard Dawson and Jane Long. Unmarried. Eton and Sandhurst. Claud Hamilton, 10 February 1913. Soldier. Captain, 3rd Battalion, Coldstream Guards. Killed at Zillebeke in the First Battle of Ypres by a high explosive shell that landed 50 yards from him. Buried Zillebeke Churchyard (E 6).

EGERTON, George Algernon.* 1 December 1870–13 May 1915. The Hon. Algernon Egerton and Alice Cavendish. Unmarried. Eton and Sandhurst. Algernon Egerton, [illegible] 1896. Soldier. Lieutenant-Colonel, 19th (Queen Alexandra's Own) Royal Hussars. Died at Battle of Frezenberg Ridge in the Second Battle of Ypres. Buried Bailleul Communal Cemetery (I 6).

ELCHO Lord, Hugo ('Ego') Francis Wemyss-Charteris-Douglas.* 28 December 1884–23 April 1916. Hugo, 11th Earl of Wemyss and Mary Wyndham. Lady Violet Manners. Eton and Trinity College, Oxford. Arthur James Balfour, 12 February 1915. Barrister. Captain, Royal Gloucestershire Hussars. Killed by shell-fire at the Battle of Katia in the Sinai desert. No known grave: Jerusalem Memorial, Jerusalem War Cemetery.

EVANS-FREKE, the Hon. Percy Cecil.* 19 May 1871–13 May 1915. William Evans-Freke, 8th Baron Carbery, and Victoria Cecil. Eva Maitland-Kirwan. Eton. [Missing]. Land agent. Lieutenant-Colonel, Leicestershire Yeomanry. Killed by two shots from a German sniper at Frezenberg Ridge in the Second Battle of Ypres when returning to RHQ after visiting a forward squadron. Buried Divisional Cemetery Ypres (E 5).

FARQUHAR, Francis Douglas, DSO.* 17 September 1874–20 March 1915. Sir Henry Farquhar, Bt, and the Hon. Alice Brand. Lady Evelyn Hely-Hutchinson. Eton. General Sir R. Pole Carew, 19 February 1907. Soldier. Lieutenant-Colonel, Coldstream Guards commanding the Princess Patricia's Canadian Light Infantry. Died at St Eloi having been hit by sniper fire while showing a relieving officer a planned line of defence. Buried Voormezeele Enclosure No 3, Ypres (Plot III, Row A, Grave 6).

FISHER-ROWE, Laurence Rowe.* 2 October 1866–13 March 1915. Captain Edward Fisher-Rowe and Edith Adams. Eveleen Hamilton-Fletcher. Eton. [Missing]. Soldier. Lieutenant-Colonel, 1st Battalion, Grenadier Guards. Killed while commanding the 1st Battalion leading up reserve companies at the Battle of Neuve-Chapelle. Buried Estaires Communal Cemetery and Extension (Plot II, Row F, Grave 9).

FITZCLARENCE, Augustus Arthur Cornwallis. 16 March 1880–28 June 1915. Henry FitzClarence and Mary Parsons. Lady Susan Yorke. Radley. John H. Ponsonby, 22 February 1909. Soldier. Captain, 2nd Battalion, Royal Fusiliers. Killed during the landing at Gallipoli. No known grave: Helles Memorial, Gallipoli (Panel 37A).

FLEMING, Valentine, DSO.* 17 February 1882–20 May 1917. Robert Fleming and Sarah Hindmarsh. Evelyn Rose. Eton and Magdalen College, Oxford. J. Ronald M. Macdonald, 7 February 1911. Merchant banker with Robert Fleming & Co. and Unionist MP for Henley. Major, C Squadron, Queen's Own Oxfordshire Hussars. Died having been struck by a shell at Guillemont Farm. Buried Templeux-le-Guérard British Cemetery (Plot II, Row E, Grave 40).

GIBBS, Eustace Lyle. 10 March 1885–10/11 February 1915. Major Antony Gibbs and Jane Merivale. Unmarried. Eton and Magdalen College, Oxford. Raymond J. Marker, 16 February 1914. Merchant banker with Antony Gibbs & Sons. Captain, North Somerset Yeomanry. Died of wounds received at Zillebeke. Buried Ypres Town Cemetery (Plot I, Row E2, Grave 18).

GOSSELIN, Alwyn Bertram Robert Raphael, DSO. 17 February 1883–7 February 1915. Sir Martin Gosselin and the Hon. Katherine Gerard. Unmarried. Beaumont and Sandhurst. Arthur FitzGerald, 20 February 1912. Soldier. Captain, 2nd Battalion, Grenadier Guards. Killed by shrapnel while dressing the wound of 2nd Lieutenant H.A.R. Graham, near Beuvry. Buried Cuinchy Communal Cemetery (Plot II, Row D, Grave 23).

HOWARD, Lyulph Walter Mowbray.* 21 November 1885–15 September 1915. Robert Howard and Louisa Sneyd. Unmarried. Harrow and New College, Oxford. Norfolk, 5 March 1910. Trainee architect. Lieutenant, 7th Battalion, Queen's (Royal West Surrey) Regiment. Killed by a shell in a trench at Bécourt section while investigating reports of a collapsed dug-out. Buried Norfolk Cemetery, Bécordel-Bécourt (Plot I, Row B, Grave 11).

IPSWICH Viscount, William Henry Alfred FitzRoy.* 24 July 1884–23 April 1918. Alfred FitzRoy, Earl of Euston, and Margaret Smith. Auriol Brougham. Harrow and Trinity College, Cambridge. V. Dawson, 13 February 1917. Surveyor. Lieutenant, 5th Battalion, Coldstream Guards, then No 17 Training Squadron, Royal Flying Corps. Died in a plane crash flying an R.E.8 towards the end of his pilot training course at Yatesbury, Wiltshire. Buried St Genevieve's Churchyard, Euston, Thetford, Suffolk.

LEGGE, The Hon. Gerald.* 30 April 1882–9 August 1915. William Heneage, 6th Earl of Dartmouth, and Mary Coke. Unmarried. Eton and Christ Church, Oxford. Dartmouth, 22 February 1912. Field naturalist. Captain, 7th Battalion, South Staffordshire Regiment. Killed on Hill 70 at Suvla Bay. No known grave: Helles Memorial, Gallipoli (Panel 134A).

LEVESON GOWER, William George Gresham.* 12 March 1883–9 October 1918. Arthur Leveson Gower and Caroline Foljambe. Unmarried. Eton and Christ Church, Oxford. Earl of Desart, 23 February 1912. Clerk in the Journal Office of the House of Lords. Lieutenant, 1st Battalion, Coldstream Guards. Killed by a shell while commanding a company at Awoingt in the Battle of Cambrai. Buried Awoingt British Cemetery (Plot III, Row H, Grave 1).

LUCAS 8th Baron (and 5th Lord Dingwall), Auberon ('Bron') Thomas Herbert, PC.* 25 May 1876–3/4 November 1916. The Hon.

Auberon Herbert and Lady Florence Cowper. Unmarried. Bedford Grammar School and Balliol College, Oxford. E. Stafford Howard, 5 March 1906. Politician. Captain, Hampshire Yeomanry and Royal Flying Corps. Shot down over German lines flying an FE2b on a reconnaissance mission during the Somme offensive. Honourable Artillery Company Cemetery, Ecoust-St Mein (Plot VIII, Row C, Grave 17).

MACDONALD-MORETON, Norman Charles Henry, MC. 18 July 1888–13 October 1915. Lieutenant-Colonel Augustus MacDonald-Moreton and Anna Sutton. Unmarried. Uppingham School. J. Ronald M. Macdonald, 12 February 1915. Soldier. Captain, 3rd Battalion, King's Royal Rifle Corps. Killed by sniper fire in the Second Battle of Ypres. Buried Fouquescourt British Cemetery (Plot III, Row K, Grave 1).

MACKENZIE, Kenneth Fitzpatrick. 3 June 1891–25 September 1915. William Mackenzie and Maud Higginson. Unmarried. Wellington College and Trinity College, Oxford. Charles E. Edgcumbe, 10 February 1915. Soldier. Lieutenant, 5th Battalion, Queen's Own Cameron Highlanders. Killed on the Hohenzollern Redoubt, Battle of Loos-en-Gohelle. No known grave: Dud Corner Cemetery, Loos (Special Memorial 8).

MACNEILL, Andrew Duncan. 17 July 1881–29 July 1917. Duncan Macneill and Louisa Agnew. Jean Beatson. Eton and Trinity College, Cambridge. H.E. FitzClarence, 24 February 1909. Soldier. Captain, 21st Heavy Battery, Royal Garrison Artillery. Killed in action at Loos. Buried Hospital Farm Cemetery (B 5).

MAITLAND MAKGILL CRICHTON, Charles Julian.* 5 September 1880–25 September 1915. David Maitland Makgill Crichton and Emily Drummond Bailey. Sybil Erle. Winchester and Trinity College, Cambridge. Sir Cosmo Duff Gordon, Bt, 7 February 1908. Olive grower in California and landowner in Scotland. Major, 10th Battalion, Gordon Highlanders. Killed at the foot of Hill 70 near Loos while giving orders to withdraw. No known grave: Loos Memorial (Panel 115 B).

MARKER, Raymond John, DSO.* 18 April 1867–13 November 1914. Richard Marker and the Hon. Victoria Digby. Beatrice Jackson. Eton and Sandhurst. Marquess of Winchester, 19 February 1901. Soldier. Colonel, General Staff (late Coldstream Guards). Died of wounds sustained when the headquarters of I Corps was bombarded on 4 November. Buried St Michael's Churchyard, Gittisham, Honiton, Devon.

MOLYNEUX-MONTGOMERIE, George Frederick. 18 September 1869–22 October 1915. Cecil Molyneux-Montgomerie and Eleanor Lascelles. Sybil Somerset. Eton and Sandhurst. [Missing]. Soldier. Major, 3rd Battalion, Grenadier Guards. Killed by sniper fire while supervising entrenchment work during the Battle of Loos. Buried Vermelles British Cemetery (Plot VI, Row D, Grave 22).

MOSTYN PRYCE, Hugh Beauclerk. 26 October 1881–19 March 1915. Edward Mostyn Pryce and Henrietta Beauclerk. Unmarried. Eton and Sandhurst. W. Beauclerk, 21 February 1907. Soldier. Captain, 4th Battalion, the Rifle Brigade. Killed by sniper fire while strengthening a position taken from the Germans in front of the village of St Eloi. Buried Bailleul Communal Cemetery (F 13).

NOLAN, Raymond Philip Drummond. 1 July 1883–3 November 1914. Philip Nolan and Frances Drummond. Kathleen O'Connor. Beaumont, Stonyhurst and New College, Oxford. John W. Drummond, 8 February 1911. Barrister. Lieutenant, 3rd Battalion, Royal Highlanders (Black Watch). Killed in action at Black Watch Corner on the north side of the Menin Road. No known grave: Menin Gate (Panel 37).

NUGENT, George Colborne, MVO.* 22 February 1864–31 May 1915. Sir Edmund Nugent, Bt, and Evelyn Gascoigne. Isabel Bulwer. Eton. [Missing]. Soldier. Colonel, acting Brigadier-General, commanding the 5th London Brigade. Killed by a stray bullet at Givenchy during the Second Battle of Artois. Buried Béthune Town Cemetery (Plot II, Row J, Grave 1).

DE LA PASTURE, Charles Edward. 15 September 1879–29 October 1914. Gerard, 4th Marquis de la Pasture, and Georgina Loughman. Agatha Mosley. Downside. Frederick Forestier Walker, 26 February 1912. Soldier. Captain, 1st Battalion, Scots Guards, British Expeditionary Force. Killed in an attack at Gheluvelt in the First Battle of Ypres. No known grave: Menin Gate (Panel 11).

PERCY, Algernon William ('Bobby').* 29 November 1884–31 May 1916. Lord Algernon Percy and Lady Victoria Edgcumbe. Unmarried. Educated at home and Christ Church, Oxford. Algernon M.A. Percy, 5 March 1909. Private means. Sub-Lieutenant, Royal Naval Reserve. Died in the sea after his ship, HMS *Queen Mary*, had been sunk in the Battle of Jutland. Buried Fredrikstad Military Cemetery, Norway.

PONSONBY, Gerald Maurice. 16 October 1876–31 August 1914. Revd the Hon. Maurice Ponsonby, 4th Baron de Mauley, and the Hon. Madeleine Hanbury-Tracy. Unmarried. Charterhouse. De Mauley, 21 February 1906. Soldier. Captain, 2nd Battalion, Royal Inniskilling Fusiliers. Died of wounds received at Wambaix in the Battle of Le Cateau. Buried Wambaix Communal Cemetery (1).

PRETOR-PINNEY, Charles Frederick, DSO.* 9 June 1864–28 April 1917. Frederick Pretor-Pinney and Lucy Smith. Phyllis Stuckey. Eton and Trinity College, Cambridge. [Missing]. Soldier. Lieutenant-Colonel, 13th Battalion, the Rifle Brigade. Died of wounds received on 23 April in the Battle of Arras. Buried Aubigny Communal Cemetery Extension (Plot VI, Row E, Grave 5).

RYDER, The Hon. Robert Nathaniel Dudley. 7 December 1882–30 November 1917. Henry Ryder, 4th Earl of Harrowby, and Susan Dent. Beryl Angas. Nothing known of his education. Loch, 20 February 1906. Soldier. Major, 8th King's Royal Irish Hussars. Killed by sniper fire having led his squadron through heavy fire to take up a position at Gauche Wood near Villers-Faucon in the Third Battle of Ypres. Buried Villers-Faucon Communal Cemetery Extension (Plot I, Row A, Grave 18).

ST AUBYN, The Hon. Piers Stewart.* 11 April 1871–29 October/16 November 1914. John St Aubyn, 1st Baron St Levan, and Elizabeth Townshend. Unmarried. Eton. The Hon. F. Leveson Gower, 2 March 1910. Land agent. 2nd Lieutenant, 2nd Battalion, 6th King's Royal Rifle Corps. Wounded in action, presumed dead, at Gheluvelt in the First Battle of Ypres. No known grave: Menin Gate (Panel 51).

SANDEMAN, George Amelius Crawshay.* 18 April 1883–26 April 1915. Lieutenant-Colonel George Sandeman and Amy Sandeman. Unmarried. Eton and Christ Church, Oxford. T.H. Boswall-Preston, 10 February 1908. Barrister and wine merchant and shipper. Captain, Hampshire Regiment. Killed at Zonnebeke in the Second Battle of Ypres. No known grave: Menin Gate (Panel 35).

SHAW STEWART, Patrick Houston.* 17 August 1888–30 December 1917. Major-General John Shaw Stewart and Mary Collyer. Unmarried. Eton and Balliol College, Oxford. Fellow of All Souls College, Oxford. Sir Hugh Shaw Stewart, Bt, 9 February 1915. Merchant banker with Baring Brothers. Lieutenant-Commander, acting Commander, Hood Battalion, Royal Naval Division. Killed in action at Gouzeaucourt. Buried Metz-en-Couture Communal Cemetery British Extension (Plot II, Row E, Grave 1).

STUCLEY, Humphrey St Leger. 7 June 1877–29 October 1914. Sir George Stucley, Bt, and Louisa Granville. Rose Carew. Eton. Fred W. Stopford, 10 February 1904. Soldier. Major, King's Company, 1st Battalion, Grenadier Guards. Killed in the First Battle of Ypres. Buried Zantvoorde British Cemetery (Plot VI, Row C, Grave 3).

THYNNE, Algernon Carteret, DSO. 9 April 1868–6 November 1917. Francis Thynne and Edith Sheridan. Constance Bonham, widow of Francis Philips. Charterhouse and Sandhurst. F.J. Thynne, 24 February 1903. Soldier. Lieutenant-Colonel, Royal North Devon Hussars. Killed leading his troops at the Battle of Sheria, which led to the capture of Beersheba. Buried Beersheba War Cemetery (L 60).

VERNON, George Francis Augustus Venables-, 8th Baron.*
28 September 1888–10 November 1915. George, 7th Baron Vernon,
and Frances Lawrence. Unmarried. Eton and Christ Church,
Oxford. William Warren Vernon, 23 February 1907. Foreign Office
and landowner. Captain, Derbyshire Yeomanry. Died of dysentery
contracted on active service at Gallipoli. Buried Pieta Military
Cemetery, Sliema, Malta (Plot D, Row 4, Grave 1).

Profiles

MAJOR LORD JOHN CAVENDISH, DSO

25 March 1875 – 20 October 1914

John Cavendish's father was the fourth son of the 7th Duke of Devonshire. Cavendish was commissioned into the 1st Life Guards in 1897. He served in South Africa throughout the Boer War, mostly as a signalling officer (including using a heliograph). He was present at the relief of Ladysmith and many other actions, was awarded the Distinguished Service Order and mentioned in despatches. Of the DSO he wrote to his family: 'it came as quite a surprise but I am very pleased to have it.'

On returning to England he declined an invitation to stand as Unionist candidate for Eastbourne, preferring to continue in the army. Serving with his regiment in Windsor and London, he found time for distractions from army routine, including visits to Canada, the USA, Kenya and Portuguese East Africa and, in the winter of 1903–1904, a long trip to Egypt and Khartoum, shooting on the Blue Nile. He also spent time at Monte Carlo. As well as shooting, he enjoyed cricket, golf, polo (still in the 1st Life Guards team in 1914) and riding to hounds. He was a Freemason.

In 1907 Cavendish told his older brother, Victor, who had taken over as Liberal Unionist MP for West Derbyshire on their father's death in 1891, that someday he would like to stand for Parliament, probably, like Victor, as a Unionist. However that year he was seconded to the Colonial Office for service with the West African Frontier Force. He was attached to its 2nd Northern Nigeria Regiment, which included a battalion of mounted infantry. By mid-1908 he had already suffered two bouts of malaria. In 1909 he was given the temporary rank of Major.

In autumn 1910 he rejoined his regiment, serving with them at Windsor and Hyde Park until the outbreak of war. He was promoted to Major in 1911. He may have hankered for a return to active service. In August 1914, after he received his orders for France, a (female) friend wrote to him: 'I expect you must be very excited at going – do you remember last year you were dying to fight the 'froggies' – why do men always want to fight?'

Soon after the declaration of war, a squadron of the 1st Life Guards, commanded by Cavendish, was detached to form part of the Household Cavalry Composite Regiment, assigned to the 4th Cavalry Brigade of the Cavalry Division of the British Expeditionary Force. The regiment's commander refused to allow a medical examination of any of his officers, knowing that he would himself be pronounced unfit to fight. The regiment arrived in France on 16 August.

The regiment saw action at Mons and in the retreat south, descending as far as Brie-Comte-Robert, 12 miles south-east of Paris. In a letter home Cavendish described how, like other units during the retreat, they were continually on the move with hardly any sleep. They then took part in the Battle of the Marne, the advance north and then the First Battle of the Aisne. The cavalry role at this stage was mostly in mobile reconnaissance, although they also took their turn at digging and holding front-line trenches. They suffered intensive shelling, but at this stage casualty figures were relatively low.

Cavendish commented to his family that so far the cavalry had an easy time compared with the infantry. His letters to his mother, like those of most officers in these early weeks of the war, included long lists of requests for items to make living conditions more comfortable: newspapers, books, tobacco, soap, cigars, a shaving brush, riding breeches, a khaki jacket, a cardigan, vests, pyjamas, a silk sleeping cap, a cheap strong watch, an electric torch in a leather case to carry on his belt.

In early October the BEF moved to Flanders, including the 1st Life Guards who went via St Omer to Messines, south of Ypres. Ypres after the fall of Antwerp was the last major obstacle to a German advance on Calais and Boulogne.

Early on 19 October the 1st Life Guards moved out of Messines to high ground about a mile east-north-east, where they dug into trenches near Gapaard. The next day the Germans launched their first major assault of the Battle of Ypres and an infantry attack on the ridge developed rapidly, with heavy shelling and rifle fire. The 3rd Hussars, who had been on the left of the Household Cavalry Composite Regiment, had to fall back and the Germans then enfiladed the regiment's left flank, including Cavendish's squadron. Cavendish, walking forward to his advanced troop to give a message to another officer, 'Tiny' Smith, came under fire from a Maxim gun and was shot dead. One of his troopers later wrote that under the intense fire, 'I laid across the dead corpse of Major Cavendish for 5 minutes before daring to drag myself any further back.'

The regiment had to retire and leave the body where it lay, between the lines, but arranged for the local farmer to bury it and mark the spot. In the event the Germans took the area and buried him, as an 'unknown British officer', in the nearby cemetery of Quesnoy. After the war the 41 British graves here were exhumed and Cavendish's remains were identified by his officer's clothing and regimental buttons. They were transferred to the British war cemetery at Cabaret-Rouge, the assembly place for some 7,000 graves from 100 cemeteries.

One of Cavendish's fellow officers paid tribute to him: 'What a loss he is. I do not suppose there is anyone who had fewer enemies, he was such a nice fellow to work with … He was always so steady and dependable, and everyone was devoted to him … the most silent and bravest man in the British Army and one of my greatest pals … the finest type of English gentleman that it has been my privilege to know.'

Cavendish was unmarried. The present (12th) Duke of Devonshire is Cavendish's great-grand-nephew. His papers are kept in the Chatsworth archive and his Life Guard accoutrements (helmet, breast-plate etc) are on display at Hardwick Hall.

Nigel Cox

2nd LIEUTENANT THE HONOURABLE PIERS ST AUBYN

11 April 1871 – 29 October/16 November 1914

As in so many aspects of war, there is confusion about the circumstances of the death of 2nd Lieutenant the Honourable Piers St Aubyn. All of the published accounts of his life report that he was last seen wounded in action in the First Battle of Ypres near Gheluvelt on 29 October 1914 and given up for dead two days later. However, there were reports that he had returned to his unit after that and a prolonged investigation ensued as to his likely whereabouts. Finally, on 10 November 1915, more than a year later, it was noted in his official personnel file: 'During an engagement on Nov. 16th [1914] at Ypres, this officer was last seen to be riddled by bullets and in a dying condition. The Germans gained the ground so that it was impossible for our men to bring him in. Our informant was most definite in his report.'

Piers St Aubyn, a bachelor, was no newcomer to warfare at the time of his death, at the age of 43, just months after joining the 60th Foot, the 6th King's Royal Rifle Corps, at the outbreak of the war. He was gazetted as a 2nd Lieutenant on 4 September 1914. His commission was confirmed posthumously. He had first seen service in 1900 as a Lieutenant in Thorneycroft's Horse in the Boer War, having sailed on the SS *Sunda* from the Albert Docks in March of that year.

The fifth son of the former British Liberal, then Liberal Unionist, MP, Sir John St Aubyn, the 1st Baron St Levan, Piers had five brothers and seven sisters. In civilian life, after Eton, he became in

1901 a Justice of the Peace in his native Cornwall, having been born on St Michael's Mount. He continued to live there as well as having a house in Albemarle Street, London. He was said to have maintained an interest in the affairs of his county working as a land agent and had a keen interest in hunting. Much of his time was taken up, during the season, in the years before the war, hare coursing.

Piers was a very clubbable man. Not only did he belong to The Travellers, joining in 1910, but also Bachelors' and Brooks's. Two of his brothers were also members of The Travellers. John Townshend St Aubyn, later the 2nd Lord St Levan, and Edward Steuart St Aubyn were elected in 1887, the year of their father's elevation to the peerage. John, in spite of being 56 at the outbreak of the war, served in the army until March 1918 and died at the age of 83 in 1940. Edward served in the army from 1879 to 1892, volunteered for the Boer War in 1900 and re-enlisted in 1914. In between he had worked at Smith St Aubyn, bill discounters, and Messrs Pasquali & Co., cigarette manufacturers. His income was no match for his expenditure and he was declared bankrupt, ceasing to be a member of the club in 1913. He died while sailing to India, as a member of the General Staff, when the SS *Persia* was torpedoed and sunk off Crete on 30 December 1915. A joint memorial service for Piers and Edward was held at St George's, Hanover Square, on 21 February 1916. They both have plaques in their memory on either side of a memorial window in the church on St Michael's Mount to the 15 men from the island who died in the Great War.

Robert Taylor

COLONEL RAYMOND MARKER, DSO

18 April 1867 – 13 November 1914

Raymond Marker, nicknamed 'Conk', spent nearly a decade at the turn of the century as an aide-de-camp, first to the Governor of Ceylon and next to the Viceroy of India, Lord Curzon of Kedleston. Curzon thought poorly of his ADCs – 'a set of youths interested only in polo and dancing' – and found it trying to have to lunch with them daily in Simla; the ADCs soon learnt to keep silent. Marker did not care for the Curzons' stiffness and formality or the challenges of 'satisfying viceregal whims'. He later noted that Lady Curzon's 'knack for being disagreeable to the staff certainly does not seem to have diminished, though she has always been like honey to me.'

Marker was able to leave Curzon's service to join the South African war, spending a year as a special service officer (including as a despatch rider) before being appointed ADC to Lord Kitchener, the Commander-in-Chief. He found Kitchener a more congenial master than Curzon, establishing a strong and enduring rapport.

Marker saw much action. He was awarded the Distinguished Service Order for his part in the capture of De Wet's gun and pompom in Cape Colony and mentioned three times in despatches. He was in charge at Vereeniging during the final deliberations of the Boer generals and, with another officer, brought the peace despatches to the King at Windsor in June 1902.

When Kitchener went out as Commander-in-Chief to India, he asked Marker (by now 'my dear Conk') to join him as senior ADC. His duties now included 'household worries', such as marshalling Kitchener's 'new army of 65 servants', including six who had worked for Queen Victoria but been ejected from royal service by Edward VII.

In 1903 Marker became engaged to Curzon's wife's sister, Daisy Leiter, but after a year she broke the engagement, later marrying another ADC, the Earl of Suffolk. Some suspected that Curzon had not considered Marker's country gentry background grand enough for one aspiring to be his brother-in-law. Marker left India for Staff College.

Marker became Kitchener's loyal and energetic ally in his power struggle with Curzon, notably in 1905 as Private Secretary to H.O. Arnold-Forster, the Secretary of State for War. He considered Curzon's behaviour to have been disgraceful and at Kitchener's bidding passed confidential papers to press contacts and other influential people, such as the Marchioness of Salisbury, who lobbied the Prime Minister. After the Government ruled against Curzon and he resigned, Marker returned to Kitchener's staff in India for a year.

He then served as a General Staff Officer at home, remaining close to Kitchener, who often wrote to him weekly and in frank terms, including about his future ambitions, ensuring that Marker had a special cypher for their confidential communications. He himself wrote papers about his own ideas on army reform and lobbied press contacts. Marker also assisted Kitchener in personal matters, helping to find him a house and estate in England and to expand his porcelain collection.

In 1912–13 Marker commanded the 2nd Battalion Coldstream Guards and was then appointed Assistant Quarter Master General, Aldershot Command. The Commanding Officer here was Lieutenant-General Sir Douglas Haig, whom Marker must have known in India, but they do not seem to have been close.

Following the outbreak of war Marker was appointed Assistant Adjutant and Quarter Master General, I Corps, British Expeditionary Force, under Haig's command. He served at Mons and through the retreat to the Marne and was awarded the Légion d'Honneur. During the retreat Marker did not just perform the traditional duties of a staff officer. An American journalist later described how: 'at a crossroads where, with the Germans pressing hard on all sides, two columns in retreat fell in together, uncertain which way to go. With confusion developing for want of instruction, a lone, exhausted staff officer who happened along took charge and, standing at the junction in the midst of shell fire, told each doubting unit what to do in a one-two-three alacrity of decision. His work finished, he and his red cap disappeared.'

The officer was Marker. His brother-in-law, an officer of 3 Coldstream, wrote that he had 'cheered everyone up because his boots were clean and his uniform tidy and he smiled so much and met so many friends at the crossroads that everyone concluded that the retreat was not serious.'

Marker then took part in the Battle of the Marne and the First Battle of the Aisne. He was again mentioned in despatches. In October the BEF moved north to Flanders, where, following the fall of Antwerp, Ypres was the last major town in Belgian hands. The BEF had hoped to advance north to retake Ghent and Bruges, but on 20 October the Germans launched massive attacks on a wide front, initiating the First Battle of Ypres. Their objective was to divide the French and British armies and drive through to take the French Channel ports.

At this stage I Corps' Advanced HQ was at the Château de Hooge, east of Ypres. On 29 October Haig moved it back to the 'White Château' closer to Ypres at a place to be known as 'Hellfire Corner' on the Menin road. On 31 October (sometimes considered to have been the single day of the war when the German Army came closest to defeating the BEF), Hooge was shelled as part of a fierce German onslaught, and the GOC 1st Division and five other officers there were fatally wounded. Over the next days the German guns were in action continuously and their bombardment of Ypres began in earnest. On 2 November Haig himself escaped injury when a shell brought down a heavy chandelier which narrowly missed his head. He now moved his HQ back into Ypres, but on 4 November these too were bombarded, and Marker was wounded when a shell burst outside the reporting centre. Five other staff officers were killed or wounded in this attack (though Haig did not mention this or the 2 November attack in his diary). Marker was evacuated to hospital in Boulogne, his leg was amputated, but on 13 November he died of heart failure.

Marker's widow, who had travelled with her sister to Boulogne to nurse him, brought his body back to England. After resting overnight at the Guards' Chapel, draped in the Union Flag, it was buried in Gittisham, Devon, following a quiet family funeral without military honours. Marker was again mentioned in despatches posthumously. One of his friends, later Field Marshal Lord Birdwood, wrote to Kitchener (who had hoped to bring Marker back from France to his staff at the War Office): 'He was a real good fellow … one of the very best one could ever hope to meet, and so able.'

Marker enjoyed polo, shooting and, at least as a young man, racing and amateur theatricals. At Simla he spent hours working on Curzon's garden, but this may have been duty rather than pastime. As well as The Travellers, he belonged to the Guards', Carlton, Turf and Pratt's clubs and the RAC. Marker's son, Richard Raymond Kitchener Marker, Kitchener's godson, born in 1908, died without children in 1961. The family estate at Combe, Gittisham, passed to his brother's grandson (Marker's great-nephew), Richard John Trelawny Marker.

Nigel Cox

LIEUTENANT-COLONEL LAURENCE FISHER-ROWE

2 October 1866 – 13 March 1915

'I think this life suits me if I don't get lead poisoning,' wrote home Lieutenant-Colonel L.R. Fisher-Rowe, Commanding Officer of the 1st Battalion, Grenadier Guards, on 2 December 1914. He was writing from forward trenches near Fleurbaix, northern France, having taken command of the battalion three days previously. The 1st Battalion had deployed with the British Expeditionary Force and had been engaged at the First Battle of Ypres in October 1914. The battalion had received heavy casualties: only four of 29 officers remained.

'The Old Friend', as Fisher-Rowe was widely known, was already familiar to many of the officers of the battalion. Cross-postings between the three Grenadier battalions were relatively common for officers, and a number of them had served with him as subalterns in the 3rd Battalion in the Boer War. He had acquitted himself well as a fighting officer, earning a mention in despatches. He deployed in the very early stages of the war with the Kimberley Relief Column. The Battle of Modder River was a formative lesson for the British Army in the combined power of modern firearms and trenches.

It is often difficult to infer personality from written documents, but in Fisher-Rowe's case certain themes come over clearly. His diary entries lack bombast, but show a steadiness and tendency to come to the right outcome. Fisher-Rowe's humanity is clear – junior soldiers are named, and are talked about as real people with affection. 'None of the company fell out, and I feel very fond of them.'

Fisher-Rowe took command of the battalion as the pattern of routine trench duties that came to characterise the Western Front became established. His early letters are full of enthusiasm: 'I think this life suits me if I don't get lead poisoning' catches the spirit well.

The tone changes markedly as December 1914 wears on. Talk moves to 'the infernal slush' of mud and 'frostbite'. This sets the context for the Christmas truce. This is what Fisher-Rowe wrote in letters home.

[25 December 1914] 'Davies and Diggle were coming, but I've had a letter from him to say he daren't as he is afraid the Boches are up to something. They have been too peaceful. Personally, I think they just want a bit of peace like us, and the Scots Guards I hear have arranged not to have any shooting last night or tonight. They certainly were very good to my digging party. The Kiddies met one of their mess and were talking to him. They were busy singing last night and had apparently lighted Xmas trees all along the trenches. It's a funny game, war and they are quite as much bored with it I expect as we are.'

[27 December 1914] 'The enemy did not attack as the authorities expected. In fact, they were all very peaceful. The Kiddies have been talking to the enemy and they had a joint funeral service over the men killed on 18th on Xmas Day and they have been giving over cigars and we reciprocate with Bully Beef. They say they are short of meat and tell our men they are fed up with the business. They wanted to play the Kiddies at football yesterday, but the Kiddies couldn't supply the ball. They say they want the truce to go on until after the New Year and I am sure I have no objection.'

[28 December 1914] 'The Germans sent in word this morning to say they would begin sniping at 11.30, but I don't think they want to start any more than we do.'

The romance now attributed to the Christmas truce was not known to Fisher-Rowe when he wrote these words. The authorities were clearly not enthusiastic about it, but the views of a senior officer escaped the censor's pen.

In early March 1915, 20 Brigade transferred to Estaires for the Neuve-Chapelle offensive. The Battle of Neuve-Chapelle was the first British offensive of the war. The First Army would capture the Aubers Ridge, breaking through to Lille. The initial attack progressed well, with Neuve-Chapelle captured by 10am on 10 March. However, failures in communications and logistics meant that momentum could not be sustained.

On 12 March, German forces mounted a major counter-attack. In response, 20 Brigade was ordered to mount a further operation that afternoon, which again embodied many of the failures in communication characteristic of Neuve-Chapelle. In recognition of the fact that the battalion had borne the brunt of the brigade's fighting the previous day, the Grenadiers were rotated into brigade reserve, with the Scots Guards and Borderers leading the brigade attack. The brigade was ordered to advance to the right of the Moulin du Piètre. This was conceptually simple, but in practice fraught with confusion. If most officers could recognise 'moulin' as windmill, fewer were familiar with the 'mn' abbreviation used on military maps. Of those fewer still could hope to identify the feature in a landscape that had been subject to three days of artillery fire. Furthermore, verbal instructions on the day are reported to have diverted the battalion away from following lead elements of the Scots Guards. The result, once more, was that the battalion's flank was exposed to an unidentified German machine gun position and became bogged down. Sir Frederick Ponsonby records in *The Grenadier Guards in the Great War of 1914–1918*: 'About the same time, Lieut. Colonel Fisher-Rowe, who came up with the companies in support, was struck in the head by a bullet and killed.'

Jonathan Lindley

LIEUTENANT-COLONEL FRANCIS FARQUHAR, DSO

17 September 1874 – 20 March 1915

Francis Farquhar was commissioned into the Coldstream Guards in 1896. In 1899 his Boer War service started unconventionally when he was sent to New Orleans to buy mules for his regiment. He then served as aide-de-camp to Major-General Sir Reginald Pole Carew and saw much action, winning the DSO and a mention in despatches.

In 1901 Farquhar was posted to China, just a year after the Boxer Rising, as Transport Officer of the 1st Chinese Regiment. This regiment had been formed in 1899 in the newly leased territory of Weihaiwei in Shantung (Shandong) province. Its port had quickly become a popular summer destination for the Royal Navy, with 12 ships stationed there in June 1902. The administration passed from military to civilian hands in May 1902, but officers of the garrison continued to assist. To ease the monotony of the winter months, the regiment kept a pack of harriers for hunting twice a week. Farquhar was a keen horseman and, though nearly six feet tall, reportedly rode in the Grand National as an amateur. Farquhar learnt some Chinese while at Weihaiwei.

In 1903 he returned to combat operations when he was sent to Somaliland for a year's duty as a Special Service Officer with the Somali Field Force, then engaged in military action against the Dervishes, led by the 'Mad Mullah', Mohammed Abdullah Hassan. Here he was one of four British officers trying to make effective mounted infantry of Somali levies, whom one of his colleagues considered 'very rum chaps'. The same officer wrote: 'My great pal here is Farquhar of the Coldstreams, a most excellent fellow. We live together, a small mess of two, and have great trouble with our Somali cooks and Somali 'boys' … the cooking is bad and the crockery awful but we have a very good time all the same … [under] the eternal sun and glowering sky and [with] the haze and the hot.' However the officers seemed to have found their unit's scouting and rear-guard duties frustrating, not least because of their Somalis' tendency to run away on their camels whenever they came under fire.

Farquhar was not always to be as tolerant of poor cuisine as he was in Somaliland. His wife, Lady Evelyn, though a talented painter, tapestry-worker, musician and gardener, was a notoriously bad house-keeper. It is said that he once pronounced the dinner-time leg of lamb completely inedible and threw it with some force out of the window.

After returning to regimental duties in England Farquhar was posted with his battalion to Egypt in 1906. From 1909, following Staff College, he served as a General Staff Officer at the War Office. In October 1913 he was appointed Military Secretary to HRH Prince Arthur, Duke of Connaught, Governor General of Canada. Farquhar's wife had since 1902 been a Lady-in-Waiting to the Duchess of Connaught.

Although in frequent attendance on the Governor General, notably during his extensive tours round Canada, Farquhar's role was much more than ceremonial. As the senior regular British officer in Canada he was a key link between the Imperial General Staff and the developing Canadian Army. Moreover the Duke of Connaught, himself a distinguished commander, was keenly interested in the development of Canadian forces, but considered the responsible Minister, Colonel Sam Hughes, to be 'militarily ignorant, conceited and very mad'.

At the outbreak of the war, with Canada still lacking significant regular military forces, Andrew Hamilton Gault, a businessman, offered to finance and equip a new battalion, and Farquhar helped him take this forward. He obtained agreement that it should be named the Princess Patricia's Canadian Light Infantry after the Governor General's daughter and helped mount an energetic recruiting drive, particularly aimed at Canadians who had served in the British Army. Farquhar was given command of the new regiment and, after training in Quebec and England, he arrived with it in France on 21 December 1914.

Farquhar and the Patricias first took their place on the front line on 6 January 1915 at Dickebusch, three miles south-west of Ypres. They spent most of the next 10 weeks in trenches here and at St Eloi south-east of Ypres. Here they took part in the Battle of Neuve-Chapelle, launched on 10 March 1915. This, the first major attempt by the British Army to launch an attack from the trenches, did not achieve its objectives.

During the Patricias' first four months in the line 85 officers and men were killed. Part of Farquhar's response was to promote men from the ranks, an innovative approach in the British Army of the day especially for a Guards officer. Five men were commissioned in the field in the first two months. Farquhar also innovated by forming a battalion sniping unit, which reportedly accounted for 17 enemy in two days and by sending out trench raiding parties.

At about 2.30am on 20 March, while showing the commanding officer of the regiment due to relieve the Patricias the new line of defence which he had planned, Farquhar was hit by a German sniper. He died before morning and was buried that night in the regimental cemetery outside Voormezeele, although the approach roads and neighbouring fields were under constant German fire. His death was announced by the Canadian Prime Minister, Sir Robert Borden, to the Canadian House of Commons the next day. He was again mentioned in despatches.

Sir John French noted in a despatch that the Patricias had been 'most ably organised, trained and commanded' by Farquhar. Sir Max Aitken wrote that the regiment was 'in fact … his creation … A strict disciplinarian, he was nevertheless deeply beloved in an army not always patient of discipline tactlessly asserted; he was always cheerful, always unruffled and always resourceful.' John Buchan described him as the 'kindest of friends, most whimsical and delightful of comrades and bravest of men'. A fellow-officer wrote: 'Very early in his military career he gave up many of the amusements and distractions of the circle in which he was placed and devoted himself heart and soul to the more serious side of his profession. [He] was always the most loyal and devoted companion, the staunchest of friends, the most helpful of brother officers. And to all this must be added the wit and humour of his intellect, his strong vitality and the fresh and interested opinions which he was always ready to give to those who sought his help or his advice.'

The Patricias distinguished themselves throughout the war, including at Vimy Ridge. They remain one of the three regular infantry regiments of the Canadian Army and continue to honour Farquhar's memory. A mountain of 9,500 feet on the border of British Columbia and Alberta was named after him.

Nigel Cox

CAPTAIN GEORGE SANDEMAN

18 April 1883 – 26 April 1915

In one of his stories, 'Sapper' – alias Herman Cyril McNeile – sets out to define the typical upper class Englishman of the Edwardian era as exemplified by his hero, Derek Vane. He was public school educated and a fine sportsman ('he had been in the XI at Eton'). He was independently wealthy ('possessing sufficient money to prevent the necessity of working'). He was also a total Philistine ('on literature, or art, or music his knowledge was microscopic … he regarded with suspicion anyone who talked intelligently on such subjects'). Summing him up, Sapper concluded: 'He belonged to the Breed; the Breed that has always existed in England and will always exist to the world's end.'

Stereotypes are comforting. They save us the trouble of fresh thought. To some extent we can see George Sandeman as belonging to 'The Breed', but only to a limited extent.

Born in 1883, Sandeman would have been roughly a contemporary of the fictional Derek Vane. Like him he went to Eton, and like him he was an outstanding cricketer. He was in the XI in 1901 and 1902. A formidable slow left-arm bowler, in his last year he took all 10 wickets for 22 in Winchester's first innings, and 16 for 46 in the whole match. Although he did not get his Blue at Oxford, he went on to play first-class cricket for Hampshire in 1913 and for the MCC in 1914. He also played for the Free Foresters and the Eton Ramblers.

Again like Derek Vane's, Sandeman's family was independently wealthy. The wine shipping business, which to this day bears the Sandeman name, had been founded in 1790. It was greatly expanded by our George Sandeman's grandfather and, even more dramatically, by his uncle Albert George Sandeman. The uncle was well connected in Portugal (he married a Portuguese noblewoman) and in the City of London where he became first a director of the Bank of England and then in 1895 its Governor. He became head of the firm on his father's death in 1868 and remained in charge until his own death in 1922. In 1902, the firm was registered as a private limited company but Albert ensured that its direction and shareholding remained entirely in family hands.

Our George's father was Lieutenant-Colonel George Glas Sandeman, Black Watch. On his death in 1905 George became a partner in the firm. Their premises in Pall Mall were conveniently situated for a member of The Travellers. At the same time he inherited his father's estates at Fonab, Perthshire, along with the family's London house at 34 Grosvenor Gardens. In the 1911 census he is recorded as having five servants looking after him there. On his death his estate was valued at over £230,000, about £24 million in today's money.

Now, however, we part company with Derek Vane, for Sandeman was no Philistine. Indeed he had a fine university record. Sandeman went up to Oxford in 1902 as an Exhibitioner at Christ Church where, in 1906, he got a Second in Modern History. His essay 'Calais Under English Rule' was one of two awarded the Arnold Prize in 1908 and was published by Blackwell's in the same year. Also, after going down, he wrote a second book, a biography of Metternich, which was published in 1911. At home in London he studied Law and was called to the Bar at the Inner Temple in 1913.

Sandeman had joined the militia while still an undergraduate. He was gazetted as 2nd Lieutenant, 3rd Battalion, Hampshire Regiment (Special Reserve) in 1903, promoted to Lieutenant in 1905 and Captain in 1914. He went to France in September 1914 and was attached to the 1st Battalion. He was, in fact, the first Special Reserve officer of that regiment to go to the front. He saw service on the Aisne and at the First Battle of Ypres.

On 22 April 1915, the Germans attacked the northern flank of the Ypres Salient between Poelcapelle and Bixschoote using gas for the first time. Quite unprepared for this form of attack, the two French divisions holding that sector gave way. Their retreat uncovered the left flank of the Canadian Division which was holding the central sector of the salient. It was to fill that gap that two British brigades were ordered forward. As part of that move, the Hampshire's 1st Battalion reached Wieltje, north-east of Ypres, on 25 April. From there they moved north to establish a defensive position opposite the German line which ran roughly west-east from St Julien to Gravenstafel. The next day, 26 April, the Germans renewed their attack. Sandeman was killed while rallying his men and preparing for a counter-attack.

The more one looks at Sandeman's life the more distant, in fact, it becomes from Sapper's model English gentleman. A gentleman he certainly was, but also a scholar, a published author, a fine cricketer, a barrister, a wine merchant and a soldier. In short, a true Renaissance man.

Paul Winby

LIEUTENANT-COLONEL GEORGE EGERTON

1 December 1870 – 13 May 1915

Major George Egerton was one of a number of officers fighting at the beginning of the war who had first-hand experience of modern warfare, having served with distinction in the Boer War at the start of the century. The positive mood of the public and the armed forces of the main combatant nations at the start of the war relied to some extent on an ignorance of the conditions of modern warfare. Major Egerton, like many Boer War veterans, is unlikely to have shared in the general exuberance.

He was typical of many of the officers in the British Expeditionary Force who set out for France in August and September 1914. He was born into an aristocratic family, educated at Eton and by 1914 was an experienced career soldier. Like so many officers and men of the 'old' army, he was to die in the early stages of the war in France.

George Algernon Egerton was born on 1 December 1870 to the Honourable Algernon Fulke Egerton MP and Alice Louisa Egerton, who was the daughter of Lord George Cavendish, the brother of the 7th Duke of Devonshire. His father was the third son of the 1st Earl of Ellesmere. At the time of George's birth his father was a rising Conservative politician who was the MP for Lancashire South-East. He went on to hold the office of Parliamentary Secretary to the Admiralty in the Disraeli government from 1874 to 1880. George was the third youngest of nine children and the only surviving son, his younger brother Ralph having died in January 1877 when he was not quite two months old.

The Egerton family had a long-standing and prominent connection with the Worsley area, near Manchester, and had, among other things, built and endowed the local church, St Mark's, in 1846. The church's records show that George was baptized there on 6 January 1871 by Canon St Vincent Beechey, a prominent clergyman of his day, and also a godson of Lord Nelson.

Egerton spent his early years at Worsley Old Hall, which still stands today but is now a real ale pub. He was educated at Eton and then went on to Sandhurst and was commissioned into the 19th (Queen Alexandra's Own) Royal Hussars in October 1891.

As a young officer, Egerton was comfortably off, having inherited £6,000 (equivalent to almost £700,000 in 2016) from his father who died in 1891. He was elected to The Travellers in 1896, where his family had strong connections. At the time of his election, five members of his extended family were members.

Egerton took his profession as a soldier seriously and he proved himself to be a very capable and brave officer during the hostilities in South Africa. Shortly after the Boer War broke out he was promoted to Captain and then saw extensive active service from November 1900 to May 1902, taking part in operations in Natal, the Transvaal and in the Orange River Colony. Egerton was mentioned in despatches and brevetted Major in October 1902.

Upon their return from South Africa, the 19th Hussars were based in Curragh Camp in County Kildare. By 1914, they were based at the Cavalry Barracks in Hounslow, and at the outbreak of the war they were split into three squadrons to be used as divisional cavalry and set out for France with the BEF in August and September. In April 1915 they were brought together again as part of the 9th Cavalry Brigade. In the following month the 19th Hussars were heavily involved in the Battle of Frezenberg Ridge, part of the Second Battle of Ypres. On day six of the battle, together with the 8th Brigade, the 9th was in reserve with the other brigades in the front line. The cavalry occupied a line from Bellewaerde Lake to the vicinity of Wieltje. The Germans commenced shelling at 4am on 13 May and the British line was subjected to constant bombardment followed by an infantry attack.

The German advance carried them into the British trenches, although in the afternoon a counter-attack by the 8th and 9th Brigades, including the 19th Hussars, succeeded in regaining the line in some places. The Battle of Frezenberg Ridge ended at around midnight on 13 May. It was a limited success for the Germans since they had only been able to gain a section of the salient about a thousand yards deep at its deepest, but the cost was so high in casualties that offensive operations were halted.

Egerton died at the HQ Clearing Hospital later that day of wounds probably sustained during the counter-attack. He is buried in the Bailleul Communal Cemetery. His headstone records his rank as Lieutenant-Colonel, having been given a temporary promotion on 17 October 1914.

George Egerton did not marry. Shortly after his death, his family erected a plaque in his memory in the family church, St Mark's, where it remains to this day.

Nicholas Brainsby

LIEUTENANT-COLONEL THE HONOURABLE PERCY EVANS-FREKE

19 May 1871 – 13 May 1915

Lieutenant-Colonel the Honourable Percy Evans-Freke was born in London in 1871. He was the second son of William, 8th Baron Carbery, a member of an old Irish family and a prominent figure in Rutland. Percy was commissioned in 1895 and served for 20 years in the Leicestershire Yeomanry. He succeeded Lieutenant-Colonel T.E. Harrison in 1913 in command of the regiment. He was killed in action in the Second Battle of Ypres on 13 May 1915.

Percy gained his first military distinction in the Boer War, where he served from 1900 to 1901 with the Imperial Yeomanry and won the Queen's Medal and four clasps. His younger brother, Cecil Montague, who served with the 16th Lancers, was killed in the war. Percy was part of an experiment, which never took root in the British Army, the Mounted Infantry. These units were established by Field Marshal Lord Roberts to cope with the highly mobile nature of the Boer tactics. There was need for the infantry to become more mobile, so infantrymen were trained to use the horse, not as a gallant steed of war, but as 'mere transportation', as Ford Motor once described competing cars. Many infantry units were converted to Mounted Infantry, which were known somewhat disparagingly as 'Ikonas', a word derived from the Kitchen Kaffir lingo. Inevitably, many were poor riders and were looked down on by the cavalry, who at the time were the elite of the British Army, though their days were numbered. Rudyard Kipling's poem M.I. gives a flavour of these units, which were disrupting the traditional ways of the British Army and having to beg, borrow or steal their equestrian requirements.

'That is what we are known as – we are the orphans they blame
For beggin' the loan of an 'ead-stall an' makin' a mount to the same.
'Can't even look at their 'orslines but someone goes bellerin' "Hi!
'Ere comes a burglin' Ikona! Footsack you – M. I.!"

Percy was the subject of a caricature by 'Snaffles' – alias Charles Johnson Payne – who was a regular soldier until he was discharged for ill-health in 1906. His later life criss-crossed Percy's, because he came to live in Rutland and shared his enthusiasm for hunting, which provided the subject of much of his work. The caricature of Percy is part of a private collection. At its foot is a line from Kipling's poem, which sums up the improvisatory, yet highly successful, nature of the mounted infantryman's activity.

'An' I don't know whose dam' column I'm in, nor where we're trekkin' nor why.'

The Second Battle of Ypres, 22 April to 25 May 1915, was notable for the fact that it was the first occasion on which the Germans used poison gas, which resulted in a large number of horrific injuries. The British and French soon also used gas. The Battle of Frezenberg Ridge, 8 May to 13 May, was one of the later episodes of the Second Battle of Ypres. The Princess Patricia's Canadian Light Infantry took particularly heavy casualties, losing 550 out of 700 men, giving rise to their unofficial motto: 'Holding up the whole damn line'. The

Leicestershire Yeomanry also suffered very severely and, on the last day of the battle at Frezenberg, Percy was killed early in the morning as he went forward to control the battle as Major Ricardo had been wounded. He is buried in the Divisional Cemetery to the west of Ypres.

Percy's death has been described by an eye-witness: 'I was in the fight in which Colonel Freke was killed, in fact, I had been in personal touch with him up to five minutes before I saw him fall. Things were rather hot, and I happened to be one of a small party, who, with Colonel Freke, had become detached from the main portion of the squadron who were holding a length of trench. We were in touch by signal, however, and a message came across that Major Ricardo was hit. Thereupon Colonel Freke walked out across the open to join the party in the trench about 80 yards away. He had covered the greater part of the distance when we saw he had been struck in the arm. He still went on to within five or six yards of the trench when he fell. He had been struck again. His soldier servant, who was in the trench, picked him up, but he was dead.'

Percy's death and many other casualties in the battle were not in vain. Although the town was almost completely destroyed, Ypres remained out of German hands, a vitally important result of the battle. In memory of the heroic stand by the Leicestershire Yeomanry a modest memorial of Leicestershire granite was dedicated on 13 May 2015 which is situated within 100 yards of where RHQ of the regiment was a hundred years ago. The ceremony was attended by a little over 70 descendants and the successor regiment. It is the only memorial to a yeomanry regiment in the Ypres Salient.

Apart from his military prowess, Percy was also a notable figure in Rutland. He had become a Justice of the Peace in 1896, while still in his twenties. He was a keen huntsman and served as secretary of the Cottesmore Hunt and he was a Deputy Lieutenant of his county. In 1896, he married Eva Maitland-Kirwan from Gelston Castle in Kirkcudbrightshire. Their daughter Maida married Captain Edmund Boyle, RN and had three sons. Percy and Eva lived at Bisbrooke Hall, which is still inhabited by his descendants.

Christopher Arnander

LIEUTENANT-COLONEL WILFRID ABEL SMITH, CMG

13 September 1870 – 19 May 1915

Wilfrid was born in 1870 when the Victorian Empire was at its height. Where exactly he was born is debatable and even the family was unsure. Goldings in Hertfordshire or in St James's? It was not a matter of concern, even the birthplace of Queen Elizabeth, The Queen Mother, was not entirely clear. What is certain is that he was born plain Smith with the Abel coming later. But he was well-born. His family sat at the top of society and at a time when double-barrelled or triple-barrelled names were in fashion. But its place in society was guaranteed whatever they called themselves. His father came from the Smith banking family, his mother was an Adeane.

After attending Cheam, he went to Eton before going to Sandhurst. He then took a commission in the Grenadier Guards. He was posted to the 1st Battalion in Dublin, where life was hardly onerous and leave of absence long. However here he learnt the craft of leadership and regimental soldiering. In 1898 the battalion was sent to the Sudan where he acted as Horse Transport Officer. He was at Omdurman. His role, though not glorious, was a vital one and demonstrated that, unlike most of his peers, he understood logistics. No mules, no food, no ammunition! He was awarded the Order of Medjidie (4th Class) for his efforts.

Soon after his return he was appointed aide-de-camp to William Lygon, Earl Beauchamp, Governor of New South Wales. In Sydney he met Violet Somerset, daughter of the 2nd Lord Raglan and sister of FitzRoy Somerset, a fellow Grenadier. Marriage followed in late 1900. But the bugles were calling and Wilfrid returned to undemanding regimental duty in London. How undemanding? One of Violet's laconic diary entries merely states: 'Queen died at 6.30pm, Wilfrid shot at Papplewick.' It was at this time that he joined The Travellers, at a cost of £42 for the entrance fee and subscription. However the 1902 family accounts show that his subscription was in arrears of 10 guineas, but for good reason.

By January 1902 the Boer War had reached a crucial stage and he joined the 3rd Battalion in what was in effect a pacifying operation, manning blockhouses, guarding lines of communication and 'controlling' Boer civilians. Some four months after his arrival peace was declared and he was swiftly returned home to command the King's Company of the 1st Battalion, Grenadier Guards. This post was – and is – one which has the personal stamp of the monarch upon it. It was also a clear sign that he was destined for greater things within the Grenadiers and the army as a whole. Needless to say his club arrears were settled.

Following the King's Company post, he joined the 3rd Battalion again in 1906 and remained with them until 1914, rising to become Senior Major or second-in-command. This is how Wilfrid's formative years were spent. In September 1914 he was promoted to Lieutenant-Colonel and to command of the 2nd Battalion in France.

The 2nd Battalion had been at the forefront of the British Expeditionary Force and had fought hard from Mons and thence to Ypres where Wilfrid took command. Casualties were heavy. Lord Cavan, the

Brigade Commander, wrote a special despatch commending the 2nd Battalion for enduring the hardest times of any of the four Guards battalions engaged in holding the line at the First Battle of Ypres. For exemplary command Wilfrid was awarded the CMG, and promotion to command a brigade was in prospect.

Promotion was not to come. In May 1915 he led the battalion in an attack at Festubert. Strong forward command was needed as officer casualties rose. Struck in the head by a stray round as he watched the attack from his Tactical Command post, he fell into a coma and died the following day. 'Never was a Commanding Officer more mourned by his men.' His loss was keenly felt by all ranks of the regiment.

But let us end with two insights into his character. In letters to FitzRoy Somerset, his brother-in-law, he was critical about the 'disgraceful' Christmas truce and the Scots Guards in particular. He felt they were badly led, should not have entertained a truce and said so. He brooked no nonsense and when Germans to his front attempted a truce he ordered his Indian Army gunners to shell their positions. He praised the Indians for producing the best gunning he had ever seen.

His other acerbic comment was a confidence shared only with FitzRoy. It concerns the Battle of the Aisne. 'The Irish Guards are the devil. Their discipline is nil. And it is demoralizing. I gather George Morris [their CO] was killed because he was up in the firing line because his rotten officers couldn't do.'

Why was he bitter? By this time only four other officers of his battalion who had formed up in Pirbright in July 1914 had survived. This was the end of the old Professional Army that held the line before the New Armies arrived.

Richard Nunneley

BRIGADIER-GENERAL GEORGE NUGENT, MVO

22 February 1864 – 31 May 1915

A *Spy* cartoon of 1897 shows George Nugent as the model of a pre-war officer of the Grenadier Guards – tall, slim, with swept-back hair and a twirling moustache. He was then a Captain and soon after was posted with the 3rd Battalion to garrison duty in Gibraltar. In March 1899 he was appointed as aide-de-camp to Major-General Sir Henry Colville, another Grenadier, then commanding the infantry brigade there.

In October 1899 Nugent accompanied Colville to Cape Colony as part of the troop build-up for the Boer War. Colville took command of 1st (Guards) Brigade in Lord Methuen's 1st Division and in February 1900 was promoted to command the Ninth Division. Nugent remained in South Africa as his ADC until June 1900. He saw much action and was twice mentioned in despatches. His style was also appreciated by the Guardsmen: at the Battle of Modder River in March 1900 (described by Methuen as 'one of the hardest and most trying fights in the annals of the British army'), one was heard to comment on the ADC's conduct when the British column came under withering Boer fire: 'He rides about on his ****ing white horse and don't care a **** and just says, "Let the ****ers shoot!".' Colville commented: 'Whether my ADC was correctly reported I do not know – perhaps he looked it more than said it.'

In June 1900 Colville was made the scapegoat for the cutting-off in confused circumstances and eventual surrender of a Yeomanry battalion, while Roberts was closing in on Johannesburg. Nugent had been laid up in hospital with typhoid at the time (as was Colville's other ADC), but he too now returned to London, having been promoted Major and appointed as one of the first officers of the Irish Guards, whose formation had been announced on 1 April.

Even though the first 200 officers and men of the Irish Guards – soon to be known as 'the Micks' – were all former Grenadiers, establishing a new regiment was no easy task. However by March 1901 Nugent was able to command their first King's Guard duty and later that month, on St Patrick's Day, they received their first presentation of shamrock from Queen Alexandra.

During 1901–02 Nugent was Commandant of the School of Instruction for Officers of the Auxiliary Forces. Based at Chelsea Barracks, this provided training for the part-time officers of the Militia, Yeomanry and Volunteers. His lectures on company drill were published and went through several editions. In his foreword he wrote: 'My experience is that there are no keener or more zealous officers than those of the Militia and Volunteers.'

Nugent was to command such officers in 1914 but before that he had 12 years with his new regiment. Throughout this period the Irish Guards were stationed in England at Aldershot or in London. However in 1903 they sent a party of 500 officers and men for ceremonial duties during the King's visit to Ireland and took part in a Royal Review of 10,000 troops in Phoenix Park.

Regimental duties were not necessarily very arduous at this period. Indeed, according to a history of the Micks, 'one Company Commander of the Irish Guards found it perfectly feasible to commute from Ireland and, by a little judicious juggling, could manage to hunt three or four days a week in the process.' Nugent, among other activities, edited and wrote most of the copy for the *Household Brigade Magazine*. He was charged on several occasions with arranging the pageant at the annual Military Tournament. He was also keen on amateur dramatics, joining two companies, the 'Old Stagers' and the 'Windsor Strollers'. It was later said of him that he 'was always anxious and ready to contribute to the pleasure and entertainment of the soldier'. He was appointed a Member of the Royal Victorian Order in January 1909.

In July 1913 Nugent was appointed Commandant of the Duke of York's Royal Military School at Dover but soon after the outbreak of war in 1914 he was brought back to resume command of the 5th London Brigade. 2nd London Division, of which the brigade was part, was soon selected for service on the Western Front, only the second territorial division to be sent there, and progressive training was carried out through the winter of 1914–15. Nugent's 5th London Brigade was the leading element of the division to land in France on 9 and 10 March 1915. Nugent by now had the temporary rank of Brigadier-General.

The division was soon engaged in the Second Battle of Artois, taking part in fighting at Aubers Ridge and Festubert. It sustained losses of 2,355 officers and men in the latter action. Nugent's brigade was only marginally involved in these actions, but on 31 May, during a relatively quiet period of trench-holding, he was killed by a stray bullet when returning from an inspection of his brigade. As Arthur Conan Doyle wrote in *A History of the Great War*: 'Even in times of quiet there was a continual toll exacted by snipers, bombers, and shells along the front which ran into thousands of casualties per week. The off-days of Flanders were more murderous than the engagements of South Africa.'

At the time of Nugent's death, both his sons were serving in the Guards: George with the Grenadiers (in which Nugent's father had also served) and Terence with the Irish Guards. Both survived the war. Terence, later Lord Nugent, GCVO, MC was Comptroller of the Lord Chamberlain's Office from 1936 to 1960.

Nigel Cox

CAPTAIN THE HONOURABLE ERNEST BRABAZON, DSO

22 March 1884 – 17 June 1915

Ernest Brabazon was the fourth son of the 12th Earl of Meath. The 12th Earl was responsible for the introduction of Empire Day in 1904. His four sons all fought in the war. His heir, Lieutenant-Colonel Lord Ardee, was Brigadier-General in the Irish Guards. Another son served in the Irish Fusiliers and the third son ended the war as a Lieutenant-Colonel in the Royal Air Force.

Captain the Honourable Ernest Brabazon was a professional soldier, having been commissioned in the 3rd Battalion of the Coldstream Guards in 1904 at the age of 20. He was promoted Lieutenant in 1906 and Captain in 1912 (the year of his marriage). In December 1914 he was mentioned in despatches: 'He has shown conspicuous efficiency in Staff duties and in keeping communication with a long line of many units, where communication was often difficult. He has carried and delivered messages under fire with promptness and dispatch.' For these services he received the Distinguished Service Order. He was noted for being keen on musketry and a good shot.

By spring 1915 there was already stalemate on the Western Front with opposing trenches dug in east of Ypres. The strategy of the Allies was to keep up the pressure on the German armies in Belgium and France in preparation for a major assault by the French under Joffre. A series of attacks led to costly and ineffective battles at Neuve-Chapelle, in the Ypres Salient and at Aubers Ridge in March, April and early May.

Various things became clear from these attacks. First, the Germans had developed a technique of using quite light first line trenches and heavily reinforced second line trenches with regular machine gun 'pill boxes' and deep dugouts. Second, there was a major shortage of ammunition for the British forces that was exposed by Colonel Charles Repington, the war correspondent of *The Times*, on 14 May. Repington had been given detailed information about this by Sir John French. This scandal precipitated the formation of a Coalition Government, but the much-needed munitions did not reach the front until October 1915. Sir John French remarked that it was 'simple murder to send infantry against powerful fortified entrenchments until they've been heavily hammered'. This rarely happened until adequate shells were available. Finally, it was difficult to rely on fixed means of communication and therefore the role of Staff Officers was very important.

The offensive in which Captain Brabazon lost his life near Givenchy in June was doomed for all of these reasons. At the first attack on 15 June, the Germans knew the British were coming due to the exploding of a large mine and the cessation of the artillery barrage. The element of surprise was lost. No re-enforcements were available so the front line was left stranded in captured German trenches having run out of grenades. General Haig was sufficiently concerned about the situation – and the lack of ammunition in particular – that he brought his GHQ near to the front line at Merville.

There was additional confusion on 17 June (the day Captain Brabazon was reported as dying) because it appeared that the Germans had abandoned certain trenches and it was therefore decided to put off the attack with a view to taking advantage of this and to occupy a more forward position during the night from which to launch the assault at 3.50am the next day. It became apparent, however, that the enemy had re-occupied the trenches in strength and at 4.05am it was decided to postpone the offensive until the 19th. Sir John French was also informed that General Foch had concluded his major offensive in the Artois.

This would have been a time of intense activity for a Staff Officer such as Captain Brabazon with orders and counter-orders in profusion. It was dangerous work with the enemy lines very close. He was killed when carrying out staff duties, visiting the 1st Battalion Irish Guards, by a high explosive shell when inspecting a machine gun post.

Lord Cavan, the first commander of the Guards Brigade, said of Captain Brabazon: 'We simply loved him, I can never tell you what he was to me, not only as a staff officer but as a friend. He was priceless, invaluable and never wearying in his work for the Brigade.' Colonel Drummond, in command of the Coldstream battalion, stated: 'Captain Brabazon was an exceptional individual, efficient and an outstanding staff officer. He is a great loss to this battalion.'

General Rawlinson summed up the events of 15 to 17 June: 'A feeling exists that life is being thrown away ... Are we not asking too much of our infantry?'

John Wates

CAPTAIN THE HONOURABLE GERALD LEGGE

30 April 1882 – 9 August 1915

In many ways Gerald Legge's life, born into a wealthy, aristocratic family, typified the generation that lived through the golden years of late Victorian and Edwardian England. He was the second of five children born to the Earl and Countess of Dartmouth spending his childhood at Patshull, the family seat near Wolverhampton. It was at home that he became a keen naturalist, taking a special interest in wildfowl.

Gerald enjoyed his schooldays and was an enthusiastic cricketer, giving his father, a first-class cricketer and President of the MCC, much pleasure. After Eton he learned farming in Northumberland and once, returning to Patshull carrying a nest of teal just hatching, he telegraphed ahead to several stations en route and secured a relay of hot water bottles by which means he succeeded in keeping the ducklings warm.

In 1899 he joined the 4th Lincolnshire Regiment then based at Parkhurst Barracks. In many ways army life suited him, but he found the endless drill tedious and in his letters home the only highlight seems to have been Queen Victoria reviewing the regiment at Osborne House.

He went up to Christ Church in 1901 where he made many good friends, but after obtaining his degree Gerald seemed to have no clear idea as to the career he should follow. In August 1904, shortly after coming down, his great friend Lord William Percy invited him on a shooting trip to North America. Gerald wrote pleadingly to his father: 'I am awful keen to go as it would make all the difference to both, to be together camping, so mind you don't blight two lives.'

The voyage was uneventful, other than his amazement, reported to his father, that only five or six of the first-class passengers dressed for dinner! They headed for Jackson Hole in Wyoming by way of New York. There they spent several weeks hunting elk, mountain sheep and bear. This first overseas adventure clearly inspired Gerald and his father realized that life as a gentleman farmer was not for him. Lord Dartmouth corresponded with W.R. Ogilvie-Grant of the British Museum about the proposed Ruwenzori Expedition. He agreed to Gerald joining the party. Due to funding difficulties the expedition was not able to start until October 1905 and in the meantime Gerald was able to spend time studying known birds of the area as well as discovering the techniques of taxidermy.

The party, led by R.B. Woosnam, also included R.E. Dent, D. Carruthers and the medical officer A.F.R. Wollaston. After landing at Mombasa they took the train to Kisumu and the boat across Lake Victoria to Entebbe. Thence a trek of 180 miles to Fort Portal during which Gerald was astounded by the enormous amount of game, but sadly there was no time to stop and hunt.

Having reached the mountains they made their first camp at 7,000 feet and here they started collecting birds, insects and plants. Gerald's work mainly concerned the collection of bird specimens, not an easy task in the bush, as well as their preservation involving the use of arsenic, which eventually caused Gerald considerable discomfort. Conditions in the camp were not ideal as it rained constantly and the mountains were covered in cloud much of the time. After four months they were relieved to move camp lower down in the Mbuku valley.

Gerald found it frustrating to be unable to hunt game, which was so prolific in the area. When it was decided to move to the west of the Ruwenzori on the Belgian Congo side he was ready to return home. The march to Beni was not without excitement as the Belgian officer in charge of the escort had alienated the local tribes, resulting in a running battle over three days during which three of the escort were killed. The expedition was Gerald's first introduction to Africa, which he loved and was drawn back to throughout the rest of his life.

In the following year, 1907, Gerald was in Malaya where his father had plantation interests. With his partner Aymer Maxwell they planned to develop a plantation in Java. Gerald enjoyed life as a planter, but admitted he was no businessman and after suffering continuous bouts of malaria he returned home in early 1908. In August of that year he set sail for Newfoundland where he spent three months hunting caribou before returning via Philadelphia.

In 1909 the British Museum asked R.B. Woosnam to lead an expedition to Lake Ngami, where the water was fast disappearing and Gerald agreed to join him. The trek across the waterless waste of the Kalahari, with little idea what was ahead, tested them to the limits. Writing to his friend J.G. Millais he described their arrival at the lake: 'On our arrival here we both went nearly mad with excitement as after that abominable waterless desert we suddenly turned up in a perfect heaven on earth – splendid water everywhere, beautiful palm trees, great papyrus swamps and a magnificent game country. Ducks everywhere and most of them quite new to me.' The trip was a success as they obtained a large number of specimens for the museum, but by the time they returned to Cape Town they were in a weak state and needed several weeks' rest before boarding ship for home.

For the next three years Gerald was based in England helping to run the family estates as well as being active in the local Territorials and Scouts in Staffordshire. Gerald longed for adventure and was clearly bored with his life in England. In February 1913 he wrote to his father in Africa: 'I have had an awful fit of longing for God's wild places again, since you have been away and I very much doubt that I can last out against it very much longer'. By early December he and a companion were on their way to southern Sudan to hunt the elusive oryx. Reaching Khartoum in January 1914 they took the train to El Obeid where they obtained camels and porters. From here they trekked some 90 miles to the north-west. Although hunting every day for two weeks they were unsuccessful in finding any oryx.

Gerald was determined to return the following year, but within a few months war had been declared and he was in the uniform of the South Staffordshire Regiment. The 7th (Service) Battalion was raised at Lichfield and Gerald was made temporary Captain in charge of D Company. There followed a period of training in Lincolnshire and Norfolk before embarking for the Dardanelles in July 1915.

On 1 August he writes to his father, after having spent nine days in the trenches: 'Really brutal as it may sound I can't remember ever having enjoyed nine days much more.' In spite of all the horrors around he still took delight in the natural world: 'The birds are a continual delight to me; there are not very many, but some very jolly ones.'

All his hunting expertise came into play and he mentions several duels with the very skilled Turkish snipers they were facing. His was not a gung-ho attitude, as he admits to being frightened, but rather a realisation of doing the best he could for the men under his command in very difficult circumstances.

On 5 August, the day before they landed at Suvla Bay and four days before he was killed, he wrote to his old friend Jack Cobbold: 'I wish we could get done with this old war all the same, I long for the old life again, but I suppose it can never be the same again with all those good fellows away. Did you hear that Woosnam was killed out here? That is the greatest loss I have had in the war. After all he and I have been through together it seems hard for him to go out like that.'

In the early hours of 9 August the battalion attacked Hill 70 and at once came under murderous fire. Within 10 minutes every single officer had either been killed or wounded. Leading D Company Gerald was hit twice in the chest and once in the knee, but was still alive and continued to exhort his men. Although completely exposed to enemy fire his devoted soldier servant Walters stayed with him to bandage his wounds, but both were shot again and died next to each other.

Gerald had little interest in social life, unless it involved sport, and there is no mention of the opposite sex in his letters other than his mother and sisters to whom he was devoted.

Johnny Millais in an appreciation wrote: 'The rising sun, the beauty of a bird's wing, or a lovely flower were things before which he stood hat in hand, just as he held everything that was false or small of no account.' Perhaps he is best described in one obituary: 'Gerald Legge was a delightful fellow, full of fun and quiet humour, a great sportsman and an ideal companion. He died as he had always lived, thinking of others.'

Richard Legge

LIEUTENANT LYULPH HOWARD

21 November 1885 – 15 September 1915

Lyulph Howard was an unlikely soldier but, when the time came, a far from reluctant one. There was no shortage of warrior genes in his lineage since he was born into a cadet branch of the Howards, Dukes of Norfolk, being the third child of Robert Mowbray Howard, great nephew of the 12th Duke. He was born at Castle Rising in Norfolk (given to the Howards by Henry VIII in 1544) but was raised at his father's agricultural estate at Hampton Lodge in Surrey.

Lyulph's childhood was conventional. He had an elder brother Henry (who survived the war as a battalion commander in the Rifle Brigade) and a sister Muriel. He went to prep school in Surrey, then on to Harrow and from there in 1904 to New College, Oxford. In 1901 he was page to the Earl Marshal (the 15th Duke of Norfolk) at the coronation of Edward VII and in 1910 was a Gentleman Usher at the coronation of George V.

Lyulph spent only a short time at New College, where the college register discloses that he failed Moderations and in June 1905 'went down without a degree, to enter business', though there is no evidence that he ever went near business. In order to understand why this was it is necessary to go back to Lyulph's time at Harrow, where he met Royall Tyler and Tudor Castle.

Royall Tyler (1884–1958) was American-born but came to England to school at the age of 14 and spent the rest of his life in Europe. A man of some means, he became a scholar of Spanish history and literature, a connoisseur and collector of Byzantine art and, subsequently, a distinguished diplomat and economist. He helped to inspire and shape the Bliss Collection of Pre-Columbian and Byzantine art presently housed at Dumbarton Oaks in Washington, DC where his correspondence with Mildred Bliss is also to be found. In that correspondence Tyler refers to Lyulph Howard as 'Little Dummer', as did also, apparently, Lyulph's family and friends. 'Little' is obvious enough, since on enlistment in August 1914 Lyulph (who was also recorded as speaking fluent Spanish and French) was 5 feet 5 inches high and weighed 9 stone. The provenance of 'Dummer' is not known.

Also at Harrow was Tudor Castle (1883–1916) who went on to publish two books of poetry. He lived with Tyler in Paris in 1906 and 1907 and was referred to by him as 'the Poet'. After Harrow, Castle studied at Trinity College, Cambridge. Tyler, Lyulph and Castle were close friends and in 1912 Castle married Lyulph's sister Muriel and, somewhat improbably, was employed by their father as land agent at Hampton Lodge. Tyler attended New College, Oxford – for just one year (1902–03) – and it seems likely that this example led Lyulph to do the same. It seems that at this stage of his life he was unsure what he wanted to do and was quite easily led.

Fellow undergraduates with Castle at Trinity were Adrian Stephen (the brother of Vanessa Bell and Virginia Woolf) and Horace de Vere Cole, both of whom Lyulph got to know through Castle. Cole was a notorious socialite (and socialist), practical joker and hoaxer, eccentric and general hell-raiser (referred to by Tyler as 'the Scoundrel'). A

Cole hoax, in which Lyulph played a part, was staged in 1905 when the 'Sultan of Zanzibar' paid an official visit to Trinity College. Cole successfully posed as the Sultan (no mean feat given that Cole was himself resident at the college at the time), with Lyulph as 'Henry Lucas' his interpreter – the entourage being solemnly escorted through Cambridge by an unwitting Mayor (described by Tyler as 'a particularly revolting Spiesser [bourgeois] whose great joy in life is to slobber over distinguished visitors') and Town Clerk.

In 1904 Tyler described Lyulph (having left Oxford) as 'working at an architect's office from 9.30 to 5.30 every day, but Saturday'. The architect in question was Sir Edwin Lutyens with whom Lyulph studied at irregular intervals until his death. It is hard to know with how much enthusiasm he pursued his architectural studies and it does not seem that he ever completed them. Tyler observed: 'It is depressing to him that his family insist on his studying architecture for three years in London. All he wants is to learn French and German, and above all to live abroad.' Having said that, he could sketch competently and he was later on close terms with Augustus John.

Lyulph spent the second half of 1905 travelling with Tyler in the interior of Spain; and then in 1906, back in London and supposedly studying, Dummer joined the Scoundrel and the Poet in a further hoax (a spoof General Election husting). In 1907 and 1908 Lyulph was in Paris, studying at the Ecole des Beaux Arts and sharing Tyler's accommodation, in succession to Castle. In 1910 he stood as godfather to Tyler's first child. It does not seem that he established any form of settled or purposeful life, but he was clearly much loved by those around him. After his death Tyler wrote: 'No one could know that boy

without loving him, it was the purest joy to be with him because his
heart was the soundest and truest I have ever met.'

Lyulph was again in Paris when war broke out. Unlike some of the
Bloomsbury Group (both Duncan Grant and Adrian Stephen were
conscientious objectors) Lyulph did not hesitate but returned at
once to England to enlist. Elsina Tyler wrote: 'Little Dummer is
going to trail a pike.' After training he was gazetted 2nd Lieutenant
in the 7th Service (Volunteer) Battalion of the Queen's (Royal West
Surrey) Regiment in October 1914, being promoted Lieutenant soon
afterwards. His battalion crossed to France in July 1915. After some six
weeks at the front he was killed by a shell in the trenches near Arras
while investigating reports of a collapsed dug-out. Lyulph's friend
and brother-in-law Tudor Castle joined the same regiment and almost
exactly a year later, having also spent six weeks at the front, was killed
in action, not far from where Lyulph died.

Shortly before Lyulph embarked for France, Augustus John painted
his portrait. The comparison with an earlier photograph tells its own
story: Little Dummer had become a man. In November 1914 Elsina
Tyler wrote: 'the training has done him endless good. He is very well
in health and has actually become talkative.' After his death Royall
Tyler (who must have the final word) wrote to Mildred Bliss: 'It is an
abominable thing that Dummer should have been killed just now, for
he was having an experience new to him in every way. As you know,
he always hated work as such, so much that he never succeeded in
doing enough labour in any field to make the flowers grow. But with
this job of soldiering, his inherited sense of duty (where skulls were
being cracked – there was the place for a Howard) made him toil at it

through all the weary months of training to such purpose that he made a first rate soldier and was to have been promoted to captain on the first vacancy … It is a very welcome thought to me that at the end he was doing something with all his heart.'

Philip Vallance

MAJOR CHARLES MAITLAND MAKGILL CRICHTON

5 September 1880 – 25 September 1915

'Major Crichton is missing, and I believe there is not much hope. It is an awful shame, as he was such a ripping man and so very popular,' wrote one young subaltern on the Western Front in October 1915. Another wrote: 'We all felt that we had a man at the head of things on whom we could rely absolutely, no matter what kind of scrape we got into. He always straightened us out, and told us just exactly the right thing to do, and never once lost his temper or condemned any man wrongly. There is no one in the battalion who is liked and respected by officers and men alike.'

Charles Julian Maitland Makgill Crichton was born on 5 September 1880. His father David served in the army, the 78th Ross-shire Buffs, but had the misfortune to break his leg badly and was in poor health until his death in 1889 at the age of 35. With his mother, three older sisters and younger brother, he grew up in Ventnor, a Victorian health resort on the Isle of Wight. He attended Winchester and briefly went up to Trinity College, Cambridge before joining his father's old regiment, now the Seaforth Highlanders, stationed in Cairo.

He was however the heir to a considerable fortune, through his great-great-grandmother Mary Johnston. The Johnstons were notorious in Fife, and probably across Scotland, for their wealth and their seclusion. On the death of George Johnston on 29 December 1900, the newspapers were full of articles about the hermit's millions and trunks full of gold. No will was found, but Charles was the entailed heir and was summoned immediately from the Middle East. Under Scottish law land held in fee tail (as opposed to fee simple i.e. freehold or life interest) can be passed only to direct descendants under the rules of primogeniture. As a result he was the undisputed heir to the heritable land, i.e. immoveable property.

Charles settled into county life, attending Unionist meetings, competing in Royal & Ancient golf competitions and becoming president of Cupar lawn tennis club. He later became a member of the Royal Company of Archers, the King's Bodyguard for Scotland. Celebrations on attaining his majority were lavish. On 30 August 1901 a ball was held at Lathrisk, the former Johnston estate in Fife, with a suite of apartments erected on the lawn.

The following poem was published the next week in the *Fife News*:

> 'King Edward sits upon the throne,
> A young laird in Lathrisk,
> The old Johnston ways are gone,
> The hermitage is brisk;
> For county squires assemble there
> Who ne'er were there before,
> The sombre-looking hermitage
> Is hermitage no more.'

Next year on 15 February, Charles married Sybil Twynihoe Erle at St Mary Magdalene, Munster Square, London. The couple then travelled to America on honeymoon. Their first born son David only lived for

21 days, but he was followed by Sylvia in 1905, Charles Frederick Andrew in 1907, Douglas in 1909 and Rosemary, who was born after Charles's death in 1915.

Given the likely scrutiny the young couple would have faced in Scotland, it is not surprising that they were attracted to an expatriate lifestyle, a decision hastened by tuberculosis affecting one of the children. They chose to move to California and eventually purchased the Ellwood Ranch in Santa Barbara in 1910. This nestled in the foothills of the Santa Ynez mountains and swept down a couple of miles to the sea. The previous owner, Ellwood Cooper, had planted some 7,000 olive trees, as well as walnut and eucalyptus trees. In time he produced significant quantities of olive oil, but struggled to compete with Sicilian imports. The Crichtons continued to press olive oil, and Sybil was always very proud of the prize that they won at a competition in Paris. It seems that there was considerable travel back and forth between California and Scotland, a journey that would take two weeks: one on the transatlantic liner and one on a train crossing America.

As the lure of California became greater, Charles returned in 1914 to sell the Lathrisk estate. Just as he had completed the sale, war broke out and he rejoined the army, obtaining a commission in the Cameron Highlanders. With a view to getting to the front more quickly he transferred to the Gordon Highlanders, where he was promoted to Major in the 10th Battalion. They landed at Boulogne in July 1915, and came under orders of 44th Brigade in 15th (Scottish) Division.

The Battle of Loos was part of a wider allied offensive across Artois and Champagne. Lens was the tactical objective, being at the intersection of the British and French armies. The plan was to encircle Lens, which was well garrisoned, rather than launch a frontal assault. Loos itself was a small mining town on the outskirts of Lens, and was the direct objective of the 44th Brigade. The *Inverness Courier* provided a fulsome account of the attack on 25 September 1915, noting how the brigade leapt out of their trenches two and a half miles away, stormed three lines of barbed wire and trenches in an hour and ten minutes before capturing the town in fierce street fighting, although with heavy casualties, particularly among the officers. With orders to go as far as they could, some 300–400 men saw the enemy retreating up Hill 70 on the outskirts of town and gave pursuit, both up the hill and down the other side, in what the *Inverness Courier* described as a 'real old time Highland charge'. They were halted only by an array of machine guns in Cité St Auguste, effectively a suburb of Lens.

As Major-General Hilton, at the time a Forward Observation Officer, said of the battle, 'the real tragedy was its nearness to complete success. Those of us who reached the crest of Hill 70 were firmly convinced that we had broken through, as there seemed to be nothing ahead of us, but an unoccupied and incomplete trench system. The only thing preventing us advancing was the exhaustion of the 'Jocks', and the flanking fire. All that was needed was artillery ammunition, and some fresh infantry, but alas neither were available, and the great opportunity passed.'

Such was the situation that Charles would have surveyed, as he took charge of Hill 70 for a time, 'coolly directing operations with his walking stick' according to an eye witness, before handing over to Colonel Sandilands of the 7th Camerons. Colonel Sandilands decided the first objective was to hold the hill at all costs, and with 300–400 men down near Cité St Auguste isolated and in danger of being cut off, he ordered that they should be withdrawn. Charles, along with Major James Barron, previously a journalist on the *Financial Times* and assistant editor of the *Inverness Courier*, volunteered to go down the hill to deliver the orders. It appears they faced scathing machine gun fire, but both of them made contact with the troops at the foot of the hill. Charles was hit in the face while giving the orders and received a fatal wound moments later. Major Barron was hit four times and was captured by the Germans shortly afterwards, dying in a German field hospital two days later. The German counter-attack proved effective and in the days that followed Hill 70 and Loos were retaken, exemplifying the stalemate that resulted from many of the battles of the Western Front.

Given the ebb and flow of battle, the fate of Charles was uncertain for some time. It appears he was initially reported wounded and missing, a week later as unofficially killed, before an official announcement around a month later. His notebook was retrieved by a Sergeant Major and returned to Sybil. In November she received a letter from a German officer:

'Madam – In handing you the enclosed photos, etc, which were found on the body of the late Major Crichton, I consider it but my duty to tell you that the Major fell as a hero at the head of his battalion after having taken Hill 70, east of Loos, by assault. When the hill was retaken by us his body, and those of many of his comrades, remained in our hands. From his wound it appears that death was instantaneous, so that he has not suffered. We laid him at rest in a soldier's grave. With the expression of my sympathy. – I am Madam, yours, etc.'

At the memorial service in Monzie parish church, the Reverend H.H. Murray gave the eulogy, commenting that 'fourteen years ago there rode into this parish, on a splendid chestnut hunter, the young laird of Monzie, dowered with every manly grace that could evoke the admiration of men, and with every gift of fortune that could commend him to their goodwill … Monzie people were proud of their laird in life, how much prouder are they in the manner of his dying? Here was a man with an intense zest in life, with exuberant health, with troops of friends, with a devoted family, with great possessions, with everything to make life worth living, and yet, at duty's call, he thrust these resolutely behind him; he was obedient to his heavenly vision, and chose the flinty, blood-drenched path, which through hunger, cold and deadly pain … leads to a glorious crown at the last.'

This author, Charles's great-grandson, is proud to report that his last visit to The Travellers was in celebration of his great-grandmother, Sybil's, 100th birthday party in 1979.

David Crichton

CAPTAIN LORD VERNON

28 September 1888 – 10 November 1915

His obituary in *The Times* of 12 November 1915 records that two of the ancestors of George Francis Augustus Venables-Vernon, Richard and Walter de Vernon, came to England with William the Conqueror. Vernon is on the Seine between Paris and Rouen.

When the Derbyshire Yeomanry Cavalry was raised in 1792 'for the better protection of the country against invasion and alarm', war having broken out with revolutionary France, the then Lord Vernon was one of the subscribers. The family thereafter traditionally served in the regiment. George was commissioned in 1906 at the age of 18, and promoted to Lieutenant in June 1912.

George Vernon was born to considerable wealth. *Kelly's Handbook* of 1915 gives George's addresses as 25 Curzon Street, Mayfair, and Sudbury Hall, Derbyshire, and mentions his membership of The Travellers. The family's seat at Sudbury Hall in Derbyshire was given to the National Trust by the 10th Baron in 1967 and was used by the BBC in 1995 to film the Pemberley interiors in their production of *Pride and Prejudice*. The family also owned an estate at Poynton in Cheshire: many places and streets in the county bear the name Vernon. Both estates also derived income from coal-mining.

His childhood was not conventionally happy. His mother, the daughter of a New York banker, became mentally ill after the birth in 1889 of

George's brother Francis and went to live in the south of France. When his father died in 1898 at the age of 44, George, then only 10 but now the 8th Baron Vernon, became a ward of an aunt and lived at Poynton Towers with her and her husband. There are local stories of a repressed childhood.

George Vernon was educated at Stone House College and Eton. In August 1902 at the age of 13 he served as a page at the coronation of Edward VII at Westminster Abbey. There is a fine portrait of him in his costume at Sudbury Hall, painted by Sir James Jebusa Shannon RA.

He was proposed for membership of The Travellers on 2 December 1901, while aged 13, and elected on 23 February 1907, aged 18. Among those who signed for him was Sir Foster Cunliffe, who is also commemorated on The Travellers' War Memorial.

George Vernon followed the then common aristocratic tradition of joining the Foreign Service at his own expense. He was appointed Honorary Attaché at the Embassy at Constantinople in 1908 and at the Legation at Munich in 1909. He appears to have set out to make up for the repressions of his childhood – or to seek the regard and affection he had been deprived of – once he came into his property. A history of Poynton village says that the young Baron 'astonished the village by leading a life of lavish entertainment and frequently being fined for speeding with his new motor car. Many stories are found in Poynton folklore … about his extravagances.' In 1909 there was a two-day coming–of–age party for the entire village as well as his friends, with gun salutes, fireworks, and a feast for 3,000 on Poynton Green. Commemorative plates were produced for the occasion, decorated with his coat of arms and motto 'Vernon semper floreat'. The local history comments: 'This occasion was marred by too much drinking and bad behaviour. Many plates were skimmed over Poynton Pool and sank.' One handsome maroon-edged plate is, however, preserved at Poynton Library. The festivities were repeated at Sudbury Hall.

In the years before the war George Vernon was prominent in London society. He was a member of the group who called themselves 'the Coterie'. According to one of its members, Lady Diana Cooper (then Lady Diana Manners): 'Our pride was to be unafraid of words, unshocked by drink and unashamed of "decadence" and gambling.' She later wrote of 'that haloed band who were to die in the war and leave us, our generation and England, woebegone and maimed – Julian and Billy Grenfell, George Vernon, Edward Horner, John Manners, Patrick Shaw Stewart, Ego and Yvo Charteris, and many, many others.' And later 'the young men who were making and moulding me and would so soon be lost. The favourites were Edward Horner, Patrick Shaw Stewart, George Vernon, Denis Anson, the Grenfells, Sidney and Michael Herbert, Tommy Bouch, and Duff Cooper.'

Diana Cooper records that in the summer of 1913 'a delightful house in Venice was taken by Maud Cunard ... She asked my mother and me to stay in September. Nancy, her daughter, was there and Harry Cust and Ronald Storrs, also the Prime Minister and Margot Asquith and Elizabeth their daughter ... In another palace, once Lady Laird's, lived for a month my nearest, my very dearest friends. Fired, I think, by my accounts of Venice and her people, [more likely, as Diana must have known, by his strong affection for her] George Vernon had taken this palazzo on the Grand Canal and brought with him the Raymond

Figure 1. Lieutenant-Colonel the Honourable Percy Evans-Freke. (*Cartoon by 'Snaffles' reproduced by kind permission of Robert Boyle*)

Figure 2. Brigadier-General George Nugent, MVO. (*Cartoon by 'Spy', Vanity Fair, 12 August, 1897*)

Figure 3. Lieutenant Lyulph Howard. (*Portrait by Augustus John, reproduced by kind permission of David Karslake, Lyulph's great nephew*)

Figure 4. Charles Bruce. Gravestone in St Margaret's Churchyard, Rottingdean. The inscription reads: Charles T Bruce – Born February 21st 1865 – Died October 23rd 1915 – Greater love hath no man than this, that a man lay down his life for his friends. (*Photo by Trevor Purnell*)

Figure 5. Captain Lord Vernon. George Francis Augustus Vernon, 8th Baron Vernon (1888–1915) by Sir James Jebusa Shannon RA (Auburn 1862–London 1923). (© *National Trust Images*)

Figure 6. 2nd Lieutenant Frederick Corley. (*Photo by Jane Horner of the Caston War Memorial, Norfolk*)

Figure 7. Memorial crosses planted in Carlton Gardens for The Travellers' Fifty during The Great War Centenary Service of Remembrance on 17 July 2014. (*Photo by Subhash Chandran*)

TO THE MEMBERS AND STAFF
WHO FELL IN THE GREAT WAR

REAR-ADM SIR R K ARBUTHNOT BART	ROYAL NAVY
CAPT HON E BRABAZON D S O	COLDSTREAM GUARDS
C T BRUCE ESQUIRE	HOSPITAL COMMANDANT
COMMANDER HON R O BRIDGEMAN D S O	ROYAL NAVY
BREV-MAJOR HON G E BOSCAWEN D S O	ROYAL FIELD ARTILLERY
LIEUT A W G CAMPBELL	COLDSTREAM GUARDS
MAJOR LORD JOHN CAVENDISH D S O	1ST LIFE GUARDS
SERGT E CHITTENDEN	ROYAL FUSILIERS
LIEUT L S COKE	IRISH GUARDS
LIEUT F C CORLEY	BORDER REGIMENT
2ND LIEUT S P COCKERELL	ROYAL FLYING CORPS
MAJOR M MAKGILL-CRICHTON	GORDON HIGHLANDERS
MAJOR SIR F CUNLIFFE BART	RIFLE BRIGADE
CAPT R L DAWSON	COLDSTREAM GUARDS
COMMANDER M DASENT	ROYAL NAVY
MAJOR G A EGERTON	19TH (QUEEN ALEXANDRA'S OWN ROYAL) HUSSARS
LIEUT-COL HON P EVANS-FREKE	LEICESTERSHIRE YEOMANRY
LIEUT LORD ELCHO	GLOUCESTERSHIRE YEOMANRY
CAPT A A C FITZCLARENCE	ROYAL FUSILIERS
MAJOR V FLEMING D S O	OXFORDSHIRE YEOMANRY
LIEUT-COL F D FARQUHAR D S O	COLDSTREAM GUARDS
CAPT A GOSSELIN D S O	GRENADIER GUARDS
CAPT E L GIBBS	NORTH SOMERSET YEOMANRY
LIEUT L W M HOWARD	THE QUEENS (ROYAL WEST SURREY REGT)
LIEUT VISCOUNT IPSWICH	ROYAL FLYING CORPS
MAJOR V B KENNETT	ROYAL FLYING CORPS
LIEUT W G G LEVESON-GOWER	COLDSTREAM GUARDS
CAPT HON G LEGGE	SOUTH STAFFORDSHIRE REGT
CAPT LORD LUCAS	ROYAL FLYING CORPS
COL R MARKER D S O	COLDSTREAM GUARDS
LIEUT K F MACKENZIE	QUEENS OWN CAMERON HIGHLANDERS
CAPT N C M MORETON	KINGS ROYAL RIFLE CORPS
MAJOR G F MOLYNEUX-MONTGOMERIE	GRENADIER GUARDS
CAPT A D MACNEILL	ROYAL GARRISON ARTILLERY
LIEUT R NOLAN	BLACK WATCH
BRIG-GEN G C NUGENT M V O	IRISH GUARDS
LIEUT A W PERCY	ROYAL NAVY
CAPT C E DE LA PASTURE	SCOTS GUARDS
CAPT H B MOSTYN PRYCE	RIFLE BRIGADE
CAPT G PONSONBY	ROYAL INNISKILLING FUSILIERS
LIEUT-COL C PINNEY	RIFLE BRIGADE
LIEUT-COL L R FISHER ROWE	GRENADIER GUARDS
MAJOR HON R N D RYDER	8TH (KINGS ROYAL IRISH) HUSSARS
MAJOR H ST L STUCLEY	GRENADIER GUARDS
CAPT G A C SANDEMAN	HAMPSHIRE REGT
LIEUT-COL W R A SMITH C M G	GRENADIER GUARDS
LIEUT-COMMANDER P H SHAW STEWART	ROYAL NAVAL DIVISION
LIEUT HON PIERS S ST AUBYN	KINGS ROYAL RIFLE CORPS
LIEUT COL A C THYNNE D S O	ROYAL NORTH DEVON YEOMANRY
CAPT LORD VERNON	DERBYSHIRE YEOMANRY

Figure 8. Photo of The Travellers' War Memorial. (*Bill Knight*)

Figure 9. Major Lord John Cavendish, DSO. Lord John Cavendish astride a pony held by Lord Richard Cavendish. (*Reproduced by kind permission of Chatsworth Settlement Trustees. © Devonshire Collection, Chatsworth*)

Figure 10. Colonel Raymond Marker, DSO.
(*Photo courtesy of the Council of the National Army
Museum, London*)

Figure 11. Lieutenant-Colonel Laurence
Fisher-Rowe. (*Photo reproduced from
Sir Frederick Ponsonby,* The Grenadier
Guards in the Great War of 1914–1918,
London, Macmillan & Co., 1920)

Figure 12. Lieutenant-Colonel Francis Farquhar, DSO. (*Photo courtesy of the Princess Patricia's Canadian Light Infantry Museum and Archives, Individual Files*)

Figure 13. Captain the Honourable Gerald Legge. (*Photo © Staffordshire Regiment Museum*)

Figure 14. Major Victor Barrington-Kennett. (*Photo courtesy of Balliol College Archives, photographer unknown*)

Figure 15. Major Sir Foster Cunliffe, Bt. (*Photo reproduced by kind permission of the Provost and Fellows of Eton College*)

Figure 16. Major Valentine Fleming, DSO. (*Photo courtesy of the Fleming Family Archives*)

Figure 17. Brevet Major the Honourable George Boscawen, DSO. (*Photo courtesy of the family, photographer unknown*)

Figure 18. Lieutenant William Leveson Gower. (© *Parliamentary Archives, London, LEG/2/2/3*)

Asquiths, Billy Grenfell, Duff and his sister Sybil Hart-Davis, Denis Anson, Edward Horner, Irene Lawley and Felicity Tree. "In questa casa ogni sera è festa," a gondolier had said in answer to a newcomer's question about its "feasting presence full of light" … In spite of my poor mother's misery, it was to the Casa delle Feste I was always trying to escape. There were the young, and no authority or sobriety. There was dancing and extravagance and lashings of wine, and charades and moonlit balconies and kisses, and some amateur prize-fighting with a mattress and seconds, and a girls' sparring match and, best of all, bets on who would swim the canal first, Duff or Denis Anson, and in their evening clothes.'

In August 1914 the Derbyshire Yeomanry was mobilised as part of the Nottinghamshire and Derbyshire Mounted Brigade. George Vernon was promoted Captain and became second-in-command of B Squadron. Deployed initially to guard the east coast of England against a possible German invasion, the regiment went to Egypt in April 1915 as part of the 2nd Mounted Division to counter a Turkish move against the Suez Canal. On 10 August the Division was hastily summoned to Cairo and told that 75 per cent of each unit must proceed as quickly as possible, dismounted, to Gallipoli. They sailed on 13 August, landed at Suvla Bay on the 18th, and on the 21st were flung into the Battle of Scimitar Hill, a last, desperate and ill-starred attempt to break the Gallipoli deadlock.

The Derbyshire Yeomanry War History, 1914–1919 vividly describes the division's advance, in perfect order, in a column 16 men wide and one and a half miles long. The supporting naval bombardment ceased as they began to move, and the column disappeared into a deadly barrage of high explosive and shrapnel. Ordered to halt for two hours in the open under fire, the survivors then launched an attack in near-darkness until stopped in their tracks by 'a withering machine-gun and rifle fire at close quarters'. The attack, like all others that day and night, was a costly failure. The remnants of the Suvla force went on to the defensive for the rest of the campaign. Many, including Lord Vernon, contracted dysentery. When withdrawn on 2 and 3 November from Suvla to Mudros on the island of Lemnos, the regiment had been reduced from 1,100 to 300, of whom 150 were reporting daily for medical treatment. The *War History* was dedicated to Lord Vernon and another officer. It notes: 'Shortly before the Regiment left Mudros it received the news of Captain Lord Vernon's death at Malta from dysentery. Lord Vernon was universally popular, and there was not an officer or man in the Regiment who did not feel, and rightly, that he had lost a real friend.'

After George Vernon's death Diana Manners wrote to a mutual friend: 'Poor darling little George … No one knows what it cost him to be brave. He told me he would be woken in the night by a frozen sweat of fear and dread of being afraid. Yet Henry Bentinck, his Colonel, writes that his courage was proverbial. His fears then were unfounded; he was not more afraid than the bravest. It bears no thinking of, his dying in Malta, conscious of death and wondering if we even knew, and then, if knowing, we loved him? And, if loving him, we were not by now half-callous to loss?' George Vernon's last letter was to Diana Manners, expressing his love. It is unlikely that she loved him as much, but she was much moved by his death, as were his other friends.

While in hospital Lord Vernon, concerned at the lack of convalescent facilities in Malta for non-officer casualties, made a gift of £2,000 for the establishment of a suitable club. The Vernon United Services Club continued in operation until the withdrawal of most British forces from Malta in the 1960s.

Two manuscript letters from George Vernon are preserved in Hertfordshire County archives in a collection of letters to Ethel, Lady Desborough, whose sons, Julian and Billy Grenfell, were friends of his. He was a regular guest at her country house, Taplow Court. The first, written some time before the war, on stiff paper with embossed address, is an elegant, carefree letter of thanks following a house party. The second, in pencil on plain, flimsy paper, is headed 'Gallipoli; Derbyshire Yeomanry; c/o Base Post Office MEF [Mediterranean Expeditionary Force]; 13.viii.15'. It is a haltingly eloquent, heartfelt letter of condolence on the death of Billy on the Western Front. Julian, whose poem 'Into Battle' was at the time considered the best written in the war, had already been killed.

When Lady Desborough heard of Lord Vernon's death, she wrote a tribute to him which was printed in the *Westminster Gazette*: 'He was very rich, and very delicate, and unspoilt by either accident. For money he had no care; all he possessed was at the disposal of chance or of anyone who wanted it … He was rather changeable and capricious in tastes, but quite unchanging to his friends. Fastidious and impulsive, his most hasty and witty criticisms were annulled by his unforgettable laugh, kind and gay … He was just twenty-seven when he died. But no thought of waste can enter in with regard to a life that was devoted so gaily for an overmastering cause.'

Anthony Layden

MAJOR VICTOR BARRINGTON-KENNETT

16 June 1887 – 13 March 1916

Victor Barrington-Kennett was the third of four sons of Lieutenant-Colonel and Mrs Brackley Barrington-Kennett. He was born in London on 16 June 1887 and educated at Ludgrove then Eton, where he was a King's Scholar. He enjoyed an active school life, becoming a member of the Eton Society, the Cricket Club and for two years played for College in the St Andrew's Day Wall Game. It was said that when Victor played for College he was 'a very weighty, strong third who has been quite invaluable in rushing loose bullies and (he) kicks with great power'.

On leaving Eton, Victor was admitted to Sandhurst, but left in his first summer in favour of Balliol College, Oxford. The college archives tell us something of his character and personality: 'Even at school he was big and impressive and in some ways grown up. "He was intellectually, I suppose, behind the rest of his election," writes a friend and contemporary, "but they all looked on him from the start as a sort of god – even strong minded people. I think he was quite amazingly unspoilt by the hero-worship he got; he had an odd, native dignity, but he never carried any side." When he came up to Balliol in 1906, it was much the same. "B.K" could take, whenever he wanted to, a leading position, though he cared little about it. With all his humour and boisterousness there was an odd shyness of manner which made his fun all the more infectious; there was also a good judgment and taste which prevented him going too far.'

Surprisingly, since Victor did not row at Eton, he quickly joined the college boat club and made the first eight. According to club records, 1907 was 'an *annus mirabilis*' when, in the Torpids, the first eight were 'Head of the River' and Victor's contribution was succinctly recorded: 'No 4 was a powerful oar with a good body swing and finish'. In 1909 the college fours won the Wyfold Challenge Cup at Henley with Victor rowing at No 2 and the Hon. Julian Grenfell, the poet, at bow. Victor continued rowing throughout his time at Balliol becoming Captain of the college boat club.

He graduated in 1910 with a Third in Modern History (rowing evidently had taken a lot of his time) and after a short period as a banker in London, Victor joined The London Balloon Company, Royal Engineers, Territorial Force as a 2nd Lieutenant. At this time the controversy over the military value of 'powered flight' was subsiding and the company was beginning to train aeroplane pilots. Barely a month after joining, Victor had made his first solo flight in an aeroplane at the Royal Aero Club flying ground at Eastchurch, Isle of Sheppey. *Flight* magazine, 20 January 1912 records: 'Barrington-Kennett made what was really the "Territorial" flight of the week on Saturday, remaining in the air for nearly three quarters of an hour, doing some sharp banking and figures of eight which would easily have gained him his pilot's certificate, and considering that he has only had charge of the machine on two previous occasions he has made wonderful progress.'

On 15 March 1912 Victor qualified for Royal Aero Club Aviation Certificate No 190 and a year later when The London Balloon

Company was formally disbanded he transferred to the Royal Flying Corps, Special Reserve.

In her book *Too Close to the Sun: The Life and Times of Denys Finch Hatton*, Sara Wheeler tells that in the summer of 1913 Denys met an old friend. 'That summer Denys took to the air himself. He went up with Victor Barrington-Kennett, a huge athlete and joker from a military family and a friend from both Eton and Oxford. Over the years Denys had enjoyed many days with Victor and his three brothers at the Barrington-Kennett home in South Kensington.' In later years Denys became an accomplished pilot himself, but it appears that his first flight was with Victor. Denys was immortalised in the pages of *Out of Africa* written by Karen Blixen in 1937. It is her memoir and tells of her love affair with Denys on the farmlands of Kenya, which much later was turned into a successful film, with Robert Redford playing the part of Denys.

Originally 2nd Lieutenant Barrington-Kennett joined No 4 Squadron, but in late 1914 he transferred to the newly reformed No 1 Squadron and began training pilots under the command of Major Geoffrey Salmond. In January 1915 this squadron moved to St Omer in northern France where Victor distinguished himself as a fine pilot and was promoted to Lieutenant and then Flight Commander, with the rank of temporary Captain. At the beginning of July he was posted home to begin a spell of instructing with No 2, No 1 and No 15 Reserve Aeroplane Squadrons. Perhaps his return to England was a compassionate posting related to the death of his brother Basil who had been killed in action with the Grenadier Guards on 18 May 1915.

On 17 January 1916 Captain Barrington-Kennett was appointed Squadron Commander ('and to be Temporary Major whilst so employed') and posted to No 4 Squadron as Commanding Officer at its base in Marieux, near Amiens.

His command lasted just two months for, while pursuing a hostile aeroplane in his Bristol Scout No 4678 near the village of Serre, Major Barrington-Kennett was shot down and killed at 12.55pm on 13 March 1916. There is some confusion surrounding the exact cause of his death. There are reports that he was shot down by anti-aircraft fire, yet there is compelling evidence (*Flight*, 11 May 1916) that 'he was shot down by a German aeroplane during a fight in the air. He was flying alone when he met his death.' Max Immelmann, the German ace nicknamed the 'Blue Max', and Lieutenant Max Ritter von Mulzer teamed up to shoot down the Bristol Scout, but it was Immelmann who claimed the success as his 10th victim.

Such was the sense of chivalry between opposing officers in the two flying corps that soon after the death of Major Barrington-Kennett, a note was dropped from a German aircraft alerting the RFC of Victor's death. He was buried with dignity by these same aviators in Miraumont Communal Cemetery, close to Albert.

The final lines of the Balliol College memorial to him read: 'B.K with all his qualities of strength and courage and practical intelligence was a perfect soldier, one whose personality pervaded the Squadron. Soldiering must have been in his blood.'

At both Eton and Oxford, Victor was a great friend of George Butterworth who is perhaps best known for his song settings of A.E. Housman's poems from *A Shropshire Lad*. He was killed in the Battle of the Somme in the early hours of 5 August 1916. In a lasting tribute Butterworth dedicated the *Shropshire Lad* songs to 'Victor Annesley Barrington-Kennett'.

Although the family kept a London house they spent much of their time in a large rented property in the village of Tillington, West Sussex from 1908 until the summer of 1914. A large, brass lectern stands close to the pulpit in the beautiful village church of All Hallows. The well-rubbed inscription reads:

This lectern
is presented by his brother officers of No 1 Squadron
Royal Flying Corps in affectionate remembrance of
Victor Annesley Barrington-Kennett
Major and Squadron Commander
and as a token of their esteem and sorrow at his loss
He was killed in an aerial fight in France
on March 13th 1916
Aged 28 years
"Be Strong and of Good Courage"

Trevor Purnell

CAPTAIN LORD ELCHO

28 December 1884 – 23 April 1916

Had he lived to fulfil his potential, 'Ego' Charteris would have combined a life of privilege with that of public service. He was known as 'Ego' owing to his early mispronunciation of his first name. He was born the Honourable Hugo Francis Wemyss-Charteris-Douglas in 1884, the son of Lord Elcho and the grandson of the 10th Earl of Wemyss. Both his father and grandfather were Members of Parliament. The family had substantial estates and properties in Scotland, Gloucestershire and London.

His parents were part of the social, political and intellectual elite known as 'the Souls'. The sub-title of Angela Lambert's book is apt, *Unquiet Souls: The Indian Summer of the British Aristocracy, 1880–1918*. Many of their children, including Ego, were part of a group who called themselves 'the Coterie'. It was a small circle of friends from a small world. They were destined for high things but the majority of the men, including Patrick Shaw Stewart, also commemorated on The Travellers' War Memorial, did not survive the war.

Ego was educated at Eton and Trinity College, Oxford. Later he was an unpaid Attaché at the Embassy of Lord Bryce in Washington during 1908 and 1909. In 1911, he married Lady Violet 'Letty' Manners, daughter of the 8th Duke of Rutland. His son and heir, David (later 12th Earl of Wemyss), was born in 1912, and his second son, Martin (later the Queen's Private Secretary, Lord Charteris of Amisfield), in

1913. Ego decided to pursue a career in law, passed his exams and was called to the Bar at the Inner Temple in 1913. In 1912 he had been commissioned as a 2nd Lieutenant in the Royal Gloucestershire Hussars. This was a part-time, volunteer cavalry regiment intended to be a home defence force during wartime. 'The Gallant Glittering Gloucesters' also had a strong social side.

Ego was popular and good at cricket and golf. At Eton, his peers elected him to 'Pop'. He played for the Eton XI against Winchester in 1902 but was not picked for the more prestigious match against Harrow at Lords. He played one first-class cricket match, for Gloucestershire against Surrey, at the Oval in 1910. At Oxford he took a third-class degree. The brightest of the Coterie took Firsts. This lack of sustainable achievements, combined with his taciturnity and diffidence, reinforced the views of his contemporaries that his undoubted potential was to be a slow and steady burn rather than a flash.

In June 1914 his grandfather died and he succeeded to the courtesy title, Lord Elcho. Settled and happy, Ego was contemplating standing as a Member of Parliament. Family friends such as the Prime Minister, Herbert Asquith, and the former Prime Minister, Arthur Balfour (a leading Soul), encouraged him to do so.

When war was declared, Ego believed that his duty was to fight for his country. He mobilised with the Royal Gloucestershire Hussars on 6 August. Part of the regiment was to serve overseas. Eventually they arrived in Egypt where much to their frustration they were engaged in the defence of the Suez Canal rather than being sent to the Gallipoli Peninsula. Egypt and Cairo proved to be more social than martial.

Some officers' wives, Letty and Ego's sister Mary included, travelled to Cairo and nursed the wounded arriving from Gallipoli.

His own sense of frustration was compounded by the news of the deaths of friends and family. The first of the Coterie to fall was John Manners. He was killed on 1 September 1914 in the Grenadier Guards' rearguard action at Villers-Cotterêts during the retreat from Mons. Ego's younger brother, Yvo, also a Grenadier, was killed in a bombing raid on the Hohenzollern Redoubt on 17 October 1915, aged 19. The Coterie and its world were slowly being destroyed. In his last letter to his mother, Ego, then patrolling with his regiment east of the Suez Canal, wrote: 'Tell Papa he must write his sons off, and concentrate on his grandsons who, thank God, exist.'

The Wemyss family read a scant report in *The Times* of Tuesday 25 April 1916 that there had been fighting at Katia involving the Yeomanry Brigade. In Cairo, Letty heard the distressing news that Ego was slightly wounded, a prisoner and being marched into Turkish captivity. An officer from the Royal Gloucestershire Hussars visited Katia and confirmed that none of the bodies could have been Ego's. Expecting that Ego would be a prisoner for the duration of the war and upset but much relieved, Letty left for England to be with the family. The official casualty list, published on 2 May in *The Times*, reported that Lieutenant (he was, in fact, a Captain) Lord Elcho was 'missing, believed wounded'.

All further attempts to discover news were to no avail until 10 June when the Red Cross informed them that Ego was definitely alive and a prisoner of the Turks in Damascus. 'We were elated with joy', wrote his mother. A worrying silence then followed despite multiple enquiries. Disquiet replaced relief. Any remaining hope was abandoned when another Red Cross telegram arrived on 3 July. It cancelled the previous telegram. Ego was not alive. He was dead. He had been killed in the last moments of the fight at Katia. Confirmation was soon received in a letter from his fellow officer and brother-in-law (he had married Ego's sister Mary in Cairo), Major Tom Strickland, who was a prisoner of war himself.

The heavy morning mist over the dunes and the soft sand had concealed the Turkish forces' approach on 23 April. Over 1,000 men, with artillery and machine guns, overwhelmed 'A' Squadron of 100 men of the Royal Gloucestershire Hussars. They tried to repulse the attack with rifle fire and one machine gun. Ego was hit in the shoulder by a bullet while directing the machine gun. He had the wound dressed in the medical tent and returned to his men in the firing line.

The attack and the heat grew intense. Ego continued to direct the fire of his men and fired himself, picking up the rifles of the dead as the casualties mounted. He was blown off his feet by a shell and a piece of shrapnel tore into his thigh. Again he went to the medical tent and had his second wound bound. As he left the tent, it scored a direct hit from a Turkish shell. With others, he pulled what wounded he could out of the blazing tent and crawled back to encourage those in the firing line who were not dead or dying. He was killed one hour before the remnants of the camp surrendered. 'Lord Elcho wounded twice then shell blew out his chest, *acted magnificently*', wrote one of his men afterwards.

Ego was 31 when he was killed. His body was never found. He was posthumously mentioned in despatches for his gallantry at Katia. An appreciation of Lord Elcho was published in *The Times* on 7 July 1916: 'The most lovable of men, singular in his charm and the quality of his humour, with reserves of strength as yet uncalled on, only for few can the future have held a brighter promise. But he had faced and reckoned with the chances of the day. For him they held no shadow of disquiet.'

Over forty years later, his sister-in-law, Lady Diana Cooper wrote that Ego was 'of all men the nearest to a knight in chivalry'. But perhaps the most poignant words are those written by his mother after he marched past her with his regiment when they left for Egypt on an April evening: 'When Ego rode by there was a slight pause for a last farewell, and then, looking splendid, he rode away into the darkness.'

Justin Davies

REAR ADMIRAL SIR ROBERT ARBUTHNOT, BT, KCB, MVO

23 March 1864 – 31 May 1916

Rear Admiral Sir Robert Keith Arbuthnot was the 4th Baronet. His great-grandfather was promised a baronetcy by George IV on 24 August 1822 at a banquet given in the King's honour by the Magistrates and Town Council of Edinburgh, where William Arbuthnot presided as Lord Provost. Apparently it was customary for the Lord Provost to be knighted, but the King enjoyed his dinner so much that he made him a baronet instead. He also said that William, who had drunk very little in contrast to the King, might have supporters to his arms if he could walk round the table without support. This he did with ease and he thereby obtained the supporters that baronets do not generally enjoy.

Sir Robert was a career naval officer whose strict and inflexible manner was in contrast to the history of the baronetcy to which he succeeded in 1889. He was a stickler for discipline and insisted on following orders and regulations to the letter. In 1900 the publication of *Commander's Order Book for a Mediterranean Battleship* reinforced his reputation as a martinet. These stern characteristics were somewhat mitigated by the recognition that he would not ask anyone to do something that he himself was not prepared to do.

He had some rather modern passions, in particular physical fitness and motorcycles. He had an obsession with physical fitness that applied both to himself and his men. He was famous for contriving arduous exercises for those under his command and timing their performances with a stop watch. He himself had been a rugby three-quarter who had captained the United Services team and played for Hampshire. He was also a boxing champion, who reputedly after dinner might bring out boxing gloves and spar with his guests. He had a Sunbeam Tonneau and competed with it in the 1904 Bexhill Speed Trials. An enthusiastic member of the Motor Cycling Club, he kept his motorbike in his day cabin and engaged in long distance endurance races. In 1908, he came third in the single-cylinder class of the Isle of Man TT, and an annual rally in the Isle of Man and a TT trophy for service members are named after him.

His sense of duty did not prevent him from speaking his mind when he saw fit. In 1910, when Captain of HMS *Lord Nelson*, he made some frank remarks about the German threat that were subsequently reported in the press. These caused a German diplomatic protest. Although consequently relieved of command, his career appeared not to have suffered as he was made aide-de-camp to the King in 1911 and was promoted to Rear Admiral in 1912. In January 1915 he received command of 1st Cruiser Squadron consisting of four large, but obsolete, armoured cruisers HMS *Defence* (flying his flag), HMS *Warrior*, HMS *Duke of Edinburgh* and HMS *Black Prince*.

During the Battle of Jutland on 31 May 1916 the 1st Cruiser Squadron formed the starboard flank of the cruiser screen, ahead of the main body of the Grand Fleet. *Defence*, Sir Robert's flagship, was just to the right of the centre of the line. Rear Admiral Horace Hood commanding the 3rd Cruiser Squadron had briefly engaged light cruisers of the German 2nd Scouting Group, damaging several as they steamed away from the High Seas Fleet at high speed during the initial 'Run to the

North' stage of the battle. Sir Robert, having seen the engagement, somewhat impetuously decided to engage the German cruisers at close range before they could escape. He promptly turned his squadron in pursuit, cutting directly across the path of the 1st Cruiser Squadron commanded by Admiral Beatty. In the course of this turn first *Defence* and then *Warrior* steamed directly in front of HMS *Lion*, forcing it to turn sharply, missing collision with it by less than 200 yards.

The British battlecruisers were at that time exchanging shells with their German counterparts as they ran north, drawing the Germans towards the main body of the Grand Fleet. Sir Robert had turned into an area full of falling shells between the fleets which other ships had been striving to avoid.

At 5.47pm *Defence* and *Warrior*, the leading two ships of the squadron, spotted the German 2nd Scouting Group and opened fire. Shortly afterwards, they spotted the SMS *Wiesbaden*, a German light cruiser, and closed to engage. Sir Robert apparently planned to close at high speed with the *Wiesbaden* in order to finish her off. When the two ships reached a range of 5,500 yards from *Wiesbaden* they were spotted in turn at 6.05pm by the German battlecruiser SMS *Derfflinger* and four other German battleships who were less than 8,000 yards away.

The fire from the German ships was heavy and the *Defence* was unable to withstand the barrage. She was hit by two salvoes from the German ships that caused the aft 9.2-inch magazine to explode. The resulting fire spread through the ammunition passages to the adjacent 7.5-inch magazines which detonated in turn. *Defence* exploded at 6.20pm with the loss of all men on board including Sir Robert. Between

893 and 903 men were killed. Three of the four ships of the 1st Cruiser Squadron were lost at Jutland.

Historians have speculated as to the cause of Sir Robert's hasty and undoubtedly courageous rush towards the German Fleet: was it a consequence of an impetuous and overzealous nature or did it stem from an excessive zeal in obeying standing orders? The answer will never be known. Sir Robert was posthumously awarded the KCB. His memory is preserved on the Plymouth Naval Memorial and there is a memorial plaque in St Giles' Cathedral, Edinburgh. Perhaps appropriately, given his membership of The Travellers, there is also a hamlet named after him in Saskatchewan.

Simon Murray

SUB-LIEUTENANT ALGERNON PERCY

29 November 1884 – 31 May 1916

Algernon William Percy, known as Bobby, joined the Royal Naval Reserve as a Sub-Lieutenant on the outbreak of war at the age of 29. He had wanted to join the army, given his eight years' service with a militia battalion in the Northumberland Fusiliers, from which he retired with the rank of Lieutenant in 1910. But his poor health would not stand up to the rigours of front-line military duty and his position in the Northumberland Fusiliers had largely been due to his family's association with the regiment: his uncle was the 7th Duke of Northumberland, and his father, Lord Algernon Percy, was Lieutenant-Colonel commanding the battalion.

Bobby was educated at his parents' home, Guy's Cliffe, Warwickshire because his health was too delicate to allow him to be sent away to boarding school. His first formal education came when he went up to Christ Church in 1904, following in the footsteps of many relations over the years. As he was nearly 20 when he went to Oxford, he remained there for only one year. After that, he was a Justice of the Peace and a County Councillor in Warwickshire, where he also served on the Prison Visiting Committee and the Hospitals Committee. Outside officialdom, he was well known and popular on the hunting field.

When he secured a place in the Royal Naval Reserve, he was delighted – all the more so to be aboard a vessel at Spithead by 24 September 1914. He wrote to his uncle, the Duke: 'I am looking forward to it very much … it is a thoroughly well thought out scheme so I don't think I was wrong in taking it as I couldn't have got anything else I could have managed half so well, and I couldn't sit at home doing nothing.' He added that he felt very lucky and pleased that his parents were quite willing for him to go. The family did not have a recent tradition of serving at sea: Bobby's father, like so many Percys, had served in the Grenadier Guards and his great-uncle (Lord Henry Percy, also a member of The Travellers) had won a Victoria Cross with the same regiment at the Battle of Inkerman in 1854. However, Bobby's great-grandfather's generation included three Admirals: Josceline and William Percy had served as junior officers in the Napoleonic wars as had their cousin, the 4th Duke of Northumberland, who eventually became First Lord of the Admiralty and president of the RNLI. As a cabinet minister in the 1850s, the 4th Duke played a part in accelerating the introduction of steam power to the Royal Navy.

Bobby's first ship was the Royal Yacht Squadron's *Catania*, a fabulously luxurious steam yacht belonging to the Duke of Sutherland which had recently been requisitioned by the Admiralty for minesweeping and U-boat patrol in the Solent. He described it as 'most comfortable… but by no manner of means a hazardous expedition'. He was, however, quick to tell his uncle that they had some guns (two 6-pounders) and lots of rifles and revolvers. But it was unlikely they would see serious action.

In January 1915 Bobby transferred to HMS *Queen Mary*. It was a prime posting for an aspiring naval officer, being one of the most modern ships in the service. Completed in 1913, she was a battlecruiser (i.e. fast and lightly armoured) and therefore designed specifically for offensive action. Her eight 13.5-inch guns had already come in to play at the Battle of Heligoland Bight on 28 August 1914. Bobby's career aboard *Queen Mary* was interrupted by illness. He had to be hospitalised and then spent considerable time on sick leave. It was not until Monday 29 May 1916 that he was able to rejoin his ship two days before the Battle of Jutland. Unfortunately, in an extraordinarily intensive action during the afternoon of Wednesday 31 May, the British battlecruisers bore the brunt of German firepower. Whereas fewer than 10 per cent of British ships present at Jutland sank, a third of the battlecruisers (three out of nine) were lost. Their relatively light armour, particularly on deck and near the gun turrets, was their undoing. Terrifyingly, all three exploded – their magazines hit – and sank in minutes, killing a total of over 3,300 men. Fewer than 1 per cent of the three battlecruisers' crews survived.

In fact Bobby survived the blowing-up of *Queen Mary*. After the initial explosion, which broke the ship in two, he found himself unhurt in the water having somehow managed to get hold of a life jacket. A short time later, there was a second explosion which shook the aft of the ship as it began to roll over and sink. He was wounded slightly in the forehead by a flying splinter but, according to a surviving midshipman who was with him, he was 'quite alright'. A destroyer soon appeared to pick them up, but about fifteen swimmers, including Bobby, were missed. The officer, who wrote to Bobby's father from a German prisoner of war camp a few weeks after the action, said that when they had all become cold and affected by the oil fumes all around them, Bobby offered him his life jacket, 'for which action I shall never forget him, although I had only known him a few days'. Sometime afterwards a German destroyer picked up the officer, semi-conscious. Only one able seaman was with him. The captain of the destroyer could see no more survivors and Bobby was never seen alive again. Just 18 of *Queen Mary's* crew of 1,264 survived.

A few weeks later, Bobby's body was washed up with many others near Fredrikstad in Norway. An English lady living nearby attended a military funeral on 28 June: 'Another English lady and myself were the only ones of their own present, and as we stood by the graves we felt we were representing the mothers and wives of the brave men whose bodies we committed to the dust … All the coffins were covered with the most beautiful wreaths and flowers brought by all kinds of people. Wasn't it kind? All the bodies had lifebelts on but no discs with their names … One officer had a ring with the initials A.W.P. and a crest engraved on his gold cuff buttons … How I wished their friends could have known that the dear remains were laid carefully and kindly in consecrated soil, it would be a little comfort to their sore hearts.' By a fortunate coincidence the author of that letter's niece lived in Northumberland so Lady Algernon Percy discovered the details of her son's burial.

A senior naval officer wrote: 'He had such a gallant big heart, always battling against delicate health and never flinching from anything because of it.' Another wrote: 'His character was one of transparent truthfulness and honesty; he honestly was one of those not very common men who are absolutely incapable of a dishonourable action, and thus did us all no end of good by simply living with us.' And a friend wrote: 'He was the soul of honour and chivalry.'

Algernon Percy

COMMANDER MANUEL DASENT

13 May 1879 – 5 June 1916

The Dasent name is possibly of Huguenot origin and may be a corruption of 'De Saintes'. A number of Huguenots are thought to have settled on the island of St Kitts, adjoining Nevis, in the West Indies in the late seventeenth century. The family became planters and the father of Manuel Dasent, Sir John Roche Dasent, wrote a family history entitled *A West Indian Planter's Family: Its Rise and Fall*. Manuel's mother was the younger daughter of Admiral of the Fleet Sir Henry Codrington, a descendant of Christopher Codrington who endowed Codrington College in Barbados and after whom the Codrington Library at All Souls was named. The family history was written in St Vincent and dated April 1913, a year before Sir John died. He writes virtually nothing about his children except that he had 'two sons in the Royal Navy to carry on their name'.

Manuel, born on 13 May 1879, entered the Navy as a cadet in July 1892. His three journals as a cadet and later midshipman in the training squadron are at the National Maritime Museum. The journals are detailed but of limited interest since they mainly contain day-to-day entries of the ship's activities such as setting sails (yes, the Navy in the 1890s still used ships with a mixture of sail and steam!), coaling and cleaning ship afterwards, anchoring, monthly payments to the crew and so on. They have many neat charts. The voyages are in the Mediterranean and Black Sea (HMS *Cockatrice*) and North America and the West Indies (HMS *Crescent*, *Active* and *Pallas*). Sometimes flashes of humour appear. 2–7 August 1894: 'One thing was shown again: you have much more to fear from your own torpedo boats than the enemies.' 25 October 1900: 'Clearing a foul anchor: the stock conceived the brilliant idea of entering a lower deck port from which it could only with great difficulty be expelled.' 8 October 1899 at Patras: 'Ripping place no houses: can't spend any money: capital country for exercise.' 1 April 1900: 'Gave good certification to bad washerwoman with date in large characters.'

Two curious incidents occurred. There was an unexpected meeting, but hardly foreshadowing the future, with Lord Kitchener on 21 December 1899 when 'sent all boats to embark Lord Kitchener and belongings on board *Isis*'. Secondly and oddly, when they anchored at Charlestown, Nevis on 2 May 1896 there is no mention of the family connections with the West Indies and Nevis in particular.

Manuel was promoted to Lieutenant on 1 October 1900. His Service Record up to his promotion to Commander on 31 December 1913 shows encouraging comments by senior officers: 'very zealous' is a frequently used term. 'Zealous and intelligent: physically VG … Fond of hunting … Recommended for promotion … Most excellent officer in every respect: great zeal, tact and attention to all his duties … Will make a good captain.' However, he evidently failed to pass an exam to enable him to go abroad and qualify as a French interpreter. He was Commander (that is second-in-command) of the cruiser HMS *Duke of Edinburgh* in the Mediterranean on the outbreak of war, joining HMS *Hampshire* as Commander in May 1915. The *Duke of Edinburgh* was sunk at Jutland along with most of the armoured cruisers in the squadron of the impetuous Rear Admiral Sir Robert Arbuthnot, also commemorated on The Travellers' War Memorial. The *Hampshire* escaped damage and there is an account of her at Jutland by her Engineer Commander Arthur Cossey, written a few days before his death in the ship.

The circumstances in which *Hampshire* was lost on 5 June 1916 with virtually all hands bar twelve survivors have been told and retold many times. She was selected to take Lord Kitchener and a party, particularly munitions experts, to Archangel in an effort to keep Russia in the war against Germany and to improve Russia's capability to produce munitions. *Hampshire* was a relatively old coal-burning cruiser but she had experience of Russian waters and was undamaged after the Battle of Jutland. The loss of Kitchener was a national catastrophe and there have been great speculation and conspiracy theories about the event, involving amongst others the IRA, German spies and Kitchener's own personal enemies, who were said to have planned his assassination.

Admiral Jellicoe instructed the *Hampshire* to take a course up the west side of the Orkneys so as to provide some shelter from a north-easterly gale. In fact the wind changed so that *Hampshire* was forced to sail directly into mountainous seas and struck a mine at about 8pm that day only one and a half miles off-shore at Marwick Head. *Hampshire* lost all power and could not launch its boats, sinking in about 10 minutes. Kitchener's party and all the ship's officers, including Dasent, lost their lives: the twelve survivors, out of nearly 700 on board, managed to reach the rocky cliff shore on Carley floats. Jellicoe had regarded the route as secure and it had apparently been used by other ships previously. Although the nearby sinking had been observed from the shore and immediate messages sent for help, rescue boats were for some reason much delayed and arrived at the scene too late. There is a tower erected by local islanders in Orkney in memory of Kitchener's death and a grave monument to Manuel Dasent in Lyness Royal Naval Cemetery on Hoy.

Nicholas Roskill

MAJOR SIR FOSTER CUNLIFFE, BT

17 August 1875 – 10 July 1916

The death of Major Sir Foster Cunliffe, a renowned military historian and cricketer, at the Battle of the Somme exemplified the profound impact that the Great War had on British society, when the comfort and convention of the Edwardian years gave way to a more violent and uncertain era.

The eldest son of a wealthy family that had made its fortune in shipping in the eighteenth century, Cunliffe came from a background of inherited privilege and prosperity. His ancestors included two eighteenth-century Mayors of Liverpool and a General in the East India Company's Bengal Army. By the late nineteenth century the family had put trade aside and settled into the patterns of country gentry at Acton Park in Wrexham. A report in *The Times* describing his coming of age celebrations gives a sense of the milieu: 'The Mayor … presented Mr Cunliffe with two silver bowls and a pearl pin. Afterwards, 3,000 school children with bands paraded past the terrace. There was also a garden party at which upwards of 4,000 persons were present.'

Cunliffe thrived at Eton. A keen and gifted cricketer, he was also an active member of the Literary Society, the Eton Society and the Corps. The minutes of a debate about the strategic importance of Gibraltar suggest a precocious interest in military matters, giving a glimpse of the future historian: 'Cunliffe thought … the position of Gibraltar was certainly overrated. Ships and transports could easily pass the Rock if the batteries were kept in check by a few ironclads, and it was open to attack from Spain. He then discussed the matter of position, and the respective advantages of elevated and horizontal fire.'

While at Eton, Cunliffe once argued in a debate that: 'Playing cricket is easier than learning Thucydides, and is less trouble, so that it is consequently in no need of encouragement, while work has to be forced on many of us before we are willing to do it.' After Cunliffe went up to New College, Oxford in 1894, cricket seems to have prevailed, absorbing more of his time than his studies.

His sporting record at Oxford was impressive, continuing in the same vein he had established at Eton. He played for the university as a freshman and every year thereafter while an undergraduate, captaining the side in 1898. According to *Wisden*: 'He excelled as a left-handed medium-pace bowler, having a good length and sending down a difficult ball that came with his arm.' One of his obituaries described him as 'one of the best Oxford bowlers of recent years'.

Cunliffe took a second-class degree, but nonetheless was awarded a fellowship at All Souls in 1898 at the age of 24. Thereafter, although he continued to play first-class cricket for Middlesex and the MCC until 1903, he applied himself with more rigour to his academic endeavours. He became a renowned military historian and pre-eminent expert on the recent conflict in South Africa, on which he published an extensive and popular two-volume account *History of the Boer War*.

He was appointed Lecturer in Military History when the position was created in 1905. According to a contemporary at All Souls, Cunliffe possessed 'a breadth of view, a grasp of the nature of war, and an insight into the mainsprings of action, unsurpassed – perhaps unequalled – in English military literature'. But Cunliffe was no bookish don. In addition to his cricket, he was active in public life, as a Governor of Shrewsbury School and Justice of the Peace for Denbigh. After inheriting the baronetcy in 1905, he stood for the Conservatives in the East Denbighshire by-election of 1909, but lost to the Liberal candidate.

Cunliffe also appears to have been popular and gregarious. He was best man to Leo Amery, later Secretary of State for India under Churchill, who had been a contemporary at All Souls. Charles Oman, another Oxford historian, wrote of a journey that he and Cunliffe had planned together from Roncesvalles to Pamplona, though the war cut short their plans: 'I had no great desire to think of making it without him. Moreover, the leisure of the times before 1914 is now denied me.' Geoffrey Winthrop Young, a famous climber (and author of *The Roof-Climber's Guide to Trinity*) described Cunliffe as 'a friend as remarkable as he was attractive'.

In December 1914, at the age of 39, Cunliffe joined a service battalion as a senior Captain, leaving a life of scholarly comfort as an Oxford don for the trenches of northern France. He landed at Boulogne with the 13th Battalion, the Rifle Brigade, in July 1915. He took his sense of humour with him. An anecdote told later by a soldier under his command recalled an improvised meal at the Somme. The men had found some provisions but lacked any vessel to cook them in until one enterprising soldier relieved a local dog of his bowl for that purpose. Cunliffe, then Company Commander, found his men enjoying their meal, which he gladly shared when invited. Afterwards, when told about the provenance of his meal, he took it in good humour: 'Well, I've attended banquets and eaten off gold plate, but I don't think I've ever before eaten food cooked in a dog's saucepan.'

Cunliffe died from wounds on 10 July 1916, a few days into the Battle of the Somme and almost exactly a year after arriving in France. He was promoted to Major (temporary), but tributes after his death suggested potential for higher command. Spenser Wilkinson, a fellow military historian at All Souls, perceived Cunliffe on 'a higher intellectual plane than all but a very few officers of the army. His study of modern war was unusually wide and deep. He seemed marked out by his qualifications for counsel and command. Yet he fell in the discharge of his duty as a regimental officer.' His obituary in *The Times* concurred: 'As a soldier, he would probably have gone far, for his theoretical knowledge of strategy was unrivalled.'

Speaking at Eton about the transience of sporting glory, Cunliffe said: 'After 35, or thereabouts, Athletics do no good to us: and what becomes of us then?' These are poignant words from a man who died shortly before his forty-first birthday.

A gifted sportsman, renowned academic and a much-loved friend: Cunliffe's sacrifice was remarkable. *The Times* described 'a man of high character, great charm and warm friendships, a good landlord and a keen all-round sportsman in the best sense of the word'. Despite his privileged background, he did not lead a life of complacency or indulgence. His dedication to public service was evident from his many endeavours, perhaps most strikingly in his decision to give up the comfortable life of an Oxford don for the battlefields of France, from which he would never return.

Piers Craven

CAPTAIN LORD LUCAS

25 May 1876 – 3/4 November 1916

Auberon Thomas Herbert, or Bron Lucas as he was to become known, was born on 25 May 1876 and was the second but eldest surviving son (his elder brother Rolf pre-deceased him at the age of 10) of the Hon. Auberon Herbert, and grandson of Henry Herbert, 3rd Earl of Carnarvon. His mother was Lady Florence, daughter of George Cowper, 6th Earl Cowper.

He was educated at Bedford Grammar School where, by all accounts, he had a somewhat unremarkable career. He entered Balliol College, Oxford in 1895. A natural athlete, he was to gain a place rowing at No 7 in the university boat in two successive years and winning for Oxford in 1898.

Bron made many friends at Oxford, of whom his close circle included Raymond Asquith (son of the Prime Minister), John Buchan and Maurice Baring. He was a countryman to his soul and was known for his brooding, good looks. Tall and restless, he hated being indoors. He was a keen bird watcher, angler, shot and adored his time stalking in the Highlands. He cut a dashing figure. He was the inspiration for Peter Pienaar in Buchan's *Mr Standfast*. He was not especially interested in what he saw as the somewhat dull world of politics, although he had been a member of the Canning Club at Oxford.

After Oxford he became war correspondent for *The Times* and volunteered to go to South Africa at the outbreak of the Boer War, where he first met another life-long friend, Winston Churchill. He received a bullet wound in his foot which was badly treated and turned septic. Upon return to England, his leg had to be amputated below the knee. For an athlete and countryman, this must have been devastating for Bron and it was to prevent him from joining the army during the coming war.

His life, however, continued with no real loss of vigour or adventure. Bron succeeded his uncle, Lord Cowper, as Baron Lucas and Dingwall in 1905 and acquired the family seat at Wrest Park in Bedfordshire, which he was later to put into the service of the Ministry for War as a military hospital. Some 3,000 wounded soldiers were treated there between 1914 and 1916 and the hospital was run by his sister Nan Herbert.

He became a Liberal peer in 1906 and was successively Private Secretary to Richard Haldane, Under-Secretary of State for War, Under-Secretary at the Colonial Office and President of the Board of Agriculture and Fisheries until May 1915. He became a Privy Counsellor in 1912. In the end, Bron regarded politics as a duty rather than a calling. He was to politics as Marius was to the ruins of Carthage. Bron did not take to life in London, although not uncommonly he sought refuge with his friends at The Travellers. He always yearned for the country and the outdoors.

When Bron left the Cabinet and in spite of being in his late 30s, he decided to join the Royal Flying Corps. He became an instructor and saw active service in Egypt in November 1915 where he was mentioned in despatches. He refused two invitations to take command of 22

Squadron, believing himself too inexperienced. However, in October 1916 he became a flight Commander based at Bertangles Aerodrome, near Amiens. On 3 November, a notably windy day, he took off in a two seater FE2b, with Lieutenant Alexander Anderson, the observer, on a reconnaissance mission to provide intelligence for the continuing Somme offensive. He was never to return, having been shot down behind enemy lines at St Pierre Vaast Wood. Two German pilots were identified as shooting down Bron's plane: Lieutenant Erich Koenig and Lieutenant Max Ritter von Müller of the Jasta 2 Squadron. His death was confirmed in December 1916 and he was buried in the Honourable Artillery Company Cemetery in Ecoust- St Mein.

In his book, *The World Crisis*, his friend Winston Churchill wrote: 'I had known him since South Africa days when he lost a leg; and to know him was to delight in him. His open, gay, responsive nature, his witty ironical but never unchivalrous tongue, his pleasing presence, his compulsive smile, made him much courted by his friends of whom he had many and of whom I was one.'

Edward Lucas

LIEUTENANT-COLONEL CHARLES PRETOR-PINNEY, DSO

9 June 1864 – 28 April 1917

Lieutenant-Colonel Charles Pretor-Pinney, DSO, Commanding Officer, the 13th Battalion, the Rifle Brigade, died on 28 April 1917, following severe wounds received during the Battle of Arras five days earlier.

A professional soldier, Pretor-Pinney had twice retired and twice re-enlisted: first, to serve in South Africa during the Boer War; and for a second time on 14 October 1914, following the outbreak of the war. He was twice mentioned in despatches. His Distinguished Service Order was gazetted in the 1 January 1917 New Year's Honours List. Citations for the DSO were published in *The London Gazette* during the Great War. However, if the DSO was a King's Birthday or New Year Honour, details were not published and, as in his case, are not available.

Although born and baptized in London, Charles, the elder son of Frederick and Lucy Pretor-Pinney, grew up in Somerton, the family home from the early nineteenth century. The Pinney family, who had acquired the estate of Lower Somerton in 1803, had been great benefactors to the town, building the parish rooms and the school. There is a memorial panel to Charles in the east window of Somerton church and his name heads the list on the war memorial. The family assumed the additional name of Pretor only in 1907, although the royal licence had been granted in 1877.

Together with his younger brother Robert, Charles was educated at Eton in Marindin's House from 1878 to 1883. He shot for the Spencer Cup in 1880 and captained the school shooting VIII in 1882. In 1883, he entered Trinity College, Cambridge and then the army, as a Lieutenant in the Royal Welch Fusiliers in 1884, before transferring to the Rifle Brigade in the same year. Charles served in Gibraltar in 1885, in Egypt from 1887 to 1888, in South Africa from 1888 to 1889, in India from 1889 to 1892, then in South Africa again from 1901 to 1902. On 12 June 1894, in Langport, Somerset, Charles married Phyllis Julia Stuckey. They had no children.

Having established his reputation as a marksman as a schoolboy, in January 1890, Charles led the 3rd Battalion shooting team in Meerut where he also won the Revolver Match. In 1891, Lieutenants Slaney and Pinney returned from a shooting trip in the Central Provinces, having bagged six tigers, one bear, four buffalo, two bison and a 'few' antelope.

When war broke out, Major Pretor-Pinney immediately rejoined the Rifle Brigade at Aldershot. On 14 October 1914, he was promoted to Lieutenant-Colonel and appointed to command the newly formed 13th (Service) Battalion. Assisted by a core of regular Rifle Brigade sergeants, the battalion was able to proceed to France on 31 July 1915.

In *The history of the Rifle Brigade in the war of 1914–1918*, an officer in his battalion writes of his Commanding Officer, Lieutenant-Colonel Pretor-Pinney: 'After approximately a year's training in England, under his guidance and discipline, this Battalion already showed signs of becoming one of the finest Service Battalions of the Army. In France, after serving a quiet sector of the line, the Battalion was removed for a month to act as show Battalion to the Third Army School at Auxi-le-Château, and from there to the Somme, where on the night of 10 July 1916, Lt Col Pretor-Pinney was wounded in an attack on Pozières and was evacuated to England.'

This refers to an unfortunate incident of the sort that happens in the fog of war. The Battalion War Diary for the first days of July 1916 describes the enemy's 'heavy and continuous daily shelling from 5am, reaching its greatest intensity at about 7.30am ... Constant heavy rain fell during both day and night ... Some progress was made in deepening the trenches and in clearing the ground of the bodies of those who had fallen between the British and enemy lines during the previous six days.'

On 10 July: 'from 3.30pm to 7.30pm we were heavily shelled, casualties amounted to about 60 other ranks and 2 officers.' At 8.15pm orders were received to attack the German front line at 8.45pm 'to advance behind an artillery barrage with support on both right and left flanks as well as the rear'. At 8.45pm 'D' and 'A' Companies left their lines with orders to take the German front line, followed at 130 yard intervals by 'C' and 'D' Companies. There was a 'puzzling absence of the promised artillery barrage and flank support'. The battalion had not covered 200 yards when a runner from the Royal Fusiliers rushed up with the message that the attack had been cancelled. The Rifles were to retire to their original line.

Though The Rifles penetrated the enemy's defences, inflicted severe losses and captured 200 prisoners, their own casualties amounted to 380 other ranks and 20 officers. The officer casualties included Pretor-Pinney, whose wounds were so severe that he was evacuated to England. That a seemingly avoidable error resulted in such disastrous casualty numbers for his battalion caused Pretor-Pinney deep and lasting distress.

The history of the Rifle Brigade records: 'The Battalion was devoted to its Colonel and, when he was fit again, all efforts were made to get him to return to France. He was not a young man and he had earned his rest at home, but, as ever, duty was the first call to him. Ultimately he returned to take over Command again, rejoining the Battalion at St Pol on 27th February 1917.'

On 12 April 1917, the battalion marched to Arras. For several days they remained in billets. Field Marshal Haig's despatches on 21 April 1917 state that 'persistent high winds and indifferent visibility were such that it was found necessary to postpone operations for a further two days … The 13th Battalion The Rifles were to move forward in the rear of the 60th and would … halt in the captured German front line trenches.'

As ordered, the battalion moved forward at 4.45am on 23 April. Soon after the battle started, the enemy put down a heavy barrage of high explosives and some gas. Casualties were very heavy going through this barrage, but the men continued to advance. Just before reaching the enemy's wire, they came upon what appeared to be assembly trenches. The first wave halted in these, all the officers leading these men having been killed or wounded. The second wave of the leading company joined the first and together they pushed on through the enemy's wire into his trenches where they began to consolidate. Units had lost touch with one another. The course of events bore little resemblance to what had been planned.

By 7.15am, command of the battalion had changed no fewer than three times. Pretor-Pinney had been badly wounded early in the attack. His successors, initially Captain the Hon. R.W. Morgan-Grenville and then Captain C.N.C. Boyle, also fell. Command was to change twice more before the battalion was relieved. Major A.N.S. Jackson, DSO, was recalled from Brigade Headquarters to assume command. Relief finally came on 29 April. Battalion casualties between 20 and 29 April were: officers – 4 killed, 6 wounded; other ranks – 28 killed, 211 wounded and 19 missing.

The burial of Pretor-Pinney, who had died on 28 April of wounds received on 23 April, took place on 30 April at Aubigny, with the following short but sincere tribute from Major Jackson: 'A man of great personal courage and charm. A magnificent disciplinarian, a rifleman in every thought and action; he will always be remembered by those who served under him as a very gallant officer and gentleman.'

James Pettit

MAJOR VALENTINE FLEMING, DSO

17 February 1882 – 20 May 1917

The Times' obituary of Valentine Fleming, written by his friend Winston Churchill, hung framed and signed on the wall of his son, Ian, as he wrote the James Bond novels. This obituary, reproduced at the foot of this article, captures the essence of the man: an MP, with a focus on doing what was right rather than a narrow party politician, a highly competent and committed officer who was respected and loved by his men, a talented sportsman and a charming individual, whose company was sought out at Eton, Oxford, Westminster, the City, Henley, France and 106 Pall Mall.

Major Fleming was the eleventh member of the House of Commons to lose his life in the Great War. While Churchill described the 'violence of faction and the fierce tumults' of Westminster, these were but shadows compared to the reality that Valentine, known as Val, subsequently faced. In his letter of November 1914 to Winston he wrote of his impressions: 'Imagine a broad belt, ten miles or so in width, stretching from the Channel to the German frontier near Basle, which is positively littered with the bodies of men and scarified with their rude graves; in which farms, villages and cottages are shapeless heaps of blackened masonry, in which fields, roads and cottages and trees are pitted and torn and twisted by shells and disfigured by dead horses, cattle, sheep and goats, scattered in every attitude of repulsive distortion and dismemberment.'

Valentine also wrote to his wife and four children and they too corresponded with him. His children called him 'Mokie' on account of his 'smoky' pipe and, as Ian Fleming's biographer writes, 'Val became the paragon of manly virtues.' The Fleming boys ended their nightly prayers with the invocation 'Please, dear God, help me to grow up more like Mokie.' He was truthful but careful as to how he shared the realities of three horrendous years: 'Some soldiers get so tired that they fall down and go to sleep and you can only keep them awake by kicking them. The Germans have huge cannons that shoot from 4 or 5 miles away. Some shells are huge things that burst in the ground and blow a huge hole.' He called them all by their nicknames and wrote how he would like to play with them, signing off as Dada.

He served with his brother Philip with whom he travelled to Dunkirk in September 1914. Philip kept a diary of the war up to the day his brother was killed from which we can understand the rare glimpses of normality that occasionally permeated life on the front. At the outset the Oxford Yeomanry had little advance notice of their deployment such that 'all ranks brought with them everything they possessed, and the officers brought cases of up to 100lbs instead of the regulation 35lbs. Probably no regiment ever went to France accompanied by such a fleet of private cars for its own personal use.' In January 1915 the brothers were even briefly able to go for walks, play polo and listen to a gramophone that Val had brought back from England. Valentine had dinner with Churchill in St Omer during the Second Battle of Ypres, which was likely to be of a higher quality fare than the bully beef out of tins he described in letters to his family.

The true risks of war were, however, never far away. As the brothers moved through France, Philip records 'we saw the Huns advancing over the top of the Messines Ridge with our fellows retiring in front of them, under heavy shrapnel fire. We lay down and opened fire.' During a tour in the trenches to check his men were under cover, Valentine's pipe was broken by a piece of shell. He described in a letter to his son Peter ('Peekiepoke') how 'a splinter of a shell hit me on the cap the other day, & a bullet went between my two arms as I was climbing out of a trench.' After a number of such incidents, Val was going from his squadron headquarters to the right-hand sector of the line at about 3.30am. Ten yards from the line a shell landed on the trench and his body together with the bodies of another officer and four men were found lying on top of the parapet.

The regimental history aptly records: 'No greater blow could have befallen the Regiment than the death of Major Valentine Fleming. Beloved by his many friends, worshipped by his squadron, admired and respected by all, he was a most gallant officer, a born leader of men. Deriving authority from his own ability and merit, being also a man of notable courage, he was able to control men merely by strength of character and personal example rather than by force of military discipline. Having everything at home to make life good, he set it aside utterly to serve his country.'

This is Winston Churchill's obituary of Valentine in *The Times*.

'The news will cause sorrow in Oxfordshire and in the House of Commons and wherever the member of the Henley Division was well known. Valentine Fleming was one of those younger

Conservatives who easily and naturally combine loyalty to party ties with a broad liberal outlook upon affairs and a total absence of class prejudice. He was most earnest and sincere in his desire to make things better for the great body of the people, and had cleared his mind of all particularist tendencies. He was a man of thoughtful and tolerant opinions, which were not the less strongly or clearly held because they were not loudly or frequently asserted. The violence of faction and the fierce tumults which swayed our political life up to the very threshold of the Great War, caused him a keen distress. He could not share the extravagant passions with which the rival parties confronted each other. He felt acutely that neither was wholly right in policy and that both were wrong in mood. Although he could have held the Henley Division as long as he cared to fight it, he decided to withdraw from public life rather than become involved in conflicts whose bitterness seemed so far to exceed the practical issues at stake. Friends were not wanting on both sides of the house to urge him to remain and to encourage him to display the solid abilities he possessed. It is possible we should have prevailed. He shared the hopes to which so many of his generation respond of a better, fairer, more efficient public life and Parliamentary system arising out of these trials. But events have pursued a different course.

'As a Yeomanry officer he always took the greatest pains to fit himself for military duties. There was scarcely an instructional course open before the war to the Territorial Forces of which he had not availed himself and on mobilization there were few more competent civilian soldiers of his rank. The Oxfordshire Hussars were the first or almost the first Yeomanry regiment to come under the fire of the enemy, and in the first battle of Ypres acquitted themselves with credit. He had been nearly three years in France, as squadron leader or second in command, and had been twice mentioned in dispatches when the shell which ended his life found him. From the beginning his letters showed the deep emotions which the devastation and carnage of the struggle aroused in his breast. But the strength and buoyancy of his nature were proofs against the somber realisations of his mind. He never for a moment flagged or wearied, or lost his spirits. Alert, methodical, resolute, untiring he did his work, whether perilous or dull, without the slightest sign of strain or stress to the end. "We all of us," writes a brother officer, "were devoted to him. The loss to the regiment is indescribable. He was, as you know, absolutely our best officer, utterly fearless, full of resource, and perfectly magnificent with his men." His passion in sport was deer stalking in his much loved native Scotland. He rode well and sometimes brilliantly to hounds, and was always a gay and excellent companion. He had everything in the world to make him happy: a delightful home life, active interesting expanding business occupations, contented disposition, a lovable and charming personality. He had more. He had that foundation of spontaneous and almost unconscious self-suppression in the discharge of what he conceived to be his duty without which happiness, however full, is precarious and imperfect. That these qualities are not singular in this generation does not lessen the loss of those in whom they shine. As the war lengthens and intensifies and the extending lists appear, it seems as if one watched at night a well loved city whose lights which burn so bright, which burn so true, are extinguished in the darkness one by one.'

Christopher Jones

LIEUTENANT-COMMANDER PATRICK SHAW STEWART

17 August 1888 – 30 December 1917

Patrick Shaw Stewart, if he had not been killed in action in 1917, could well have been with us for fifty more years. The most distinguished of our present members, who joined young, could have known him. Loved by his friends for his fine conversation, he would have been a star of the club table.

PSS shone brightly at Eton. He won his place in 1901 with a scholarship, coming top of his year list, the first sign that he was Very Clever. He threw himself energetically into bookwork, but games too. While various subjects were creeping into the curriculum, Classics commanded the greatest prestige. PSS drank deeply of Greek and Latin, without hard grind. He had great facility for learning and a subtle feel for language and style, along with a phenomenal memory.

Throughout Eton and Oxford he applied himself in fits and starts. Essays could be written on a train after a London ball or a weekend house-party. But show him a prize and he would prepare with intensity. He was a star among prizewinners: the Newcastle (at Eton), the Gaisford, Hertford, Ireland and Craven.

There was plenty else in his life both at Eton (which he loved) and at Balliol. Sports, socialising (all those Edwardian house-parties full of aristocrats and top politicians), speeches at the Union (his not of heavyweight quality) and high jinks. My Oxford in the 1960s was still passably good at the latter, but Etonians at Balliol in the Edwardian era were a hard act to follow. One example must suffice here. Charles Lister, a close friend of PSS, had strayed into Trinity next door to join in a riotous bonfire, had swept up a small young man and was waltzing him round in his excitement, not realising he was manhandling the Reverend Junior Dean. Balliol felt obliged to send Lister down for this. His friends, in protest, carved a mock headstone over his staircase inscribed – this was PSS's touch – with words from Acts 23.5: 'I wist not, brethren, that he was the high priest.'

Much time was spent in visits to country houses; ducal and sub-ducal houses (later, in the forces, PSS was teased as a collector of duchesses). Links were made with the great landed and political families; warm links with their extremely beautiful young ladies. For all his academic prowess, PSS was not seriously drawn to academic life. Too much love of action. But before detaching himself from Oxford he won a competition Fellowship at All Souls, rather to his surprise because the focus was on modern history, which he had barely studied. Greats, it seems, had sharpened his ability to define crucial issues lucidly and with that to mask weakness of detailed knowledge.

His entry in our candidates' book shows his profession as Fellow of All Souls, Oxford. For choice of further career he hesitated between the Bar and banking. He received an open invitation from Barings. Advice from Richard Haldane, Secretary of State for War, seems to have tipped the scales: 'The improbable possibilities of the Bar may be better than the improbable possibilities of Barings, but the probable possibilities of Barings are the best.' He was going to need good earnings to fuel his love of high living and high society. Within two years Barings made him a Managing Director, but then, before he had got much beyond first steps in office procedure and a foreign training mission or two, war came.

PSS with many of his Eton contemporaries decided to join up fast. They seem to have thought the conflict might be over in quick time, like the Franco-Prussian War. Was it zest for further honours, for more prizes, that led to such a high toll of Old Etonians?

Connections weighed in again. Churchill, by now at the Admiralty, had created an anomalous hybrid of army and navy, the Royal Naval Division, and it was to play a part at Gallipoli. PSS and several of his closest friends were attracted to this. Gallipoli: a splendid wheeze, clever distraction of the enemy, and prospects of shining in a brilliant new campaign away from the killing fields of Flanders. Churchill, who knew all these young men from house-parties, saw to it that the friends were together in one battalion, the 'Hood'.

Rupert Brooke was among them. He fell fatally ill on the journey out. PSS was in the party which buried Rupert on Skyros with military honours. These young men fresh from total immersion in the Classics naturally had Homer in their minds as they drew nearer to the scenes of the Trojan War. PSS wrote a fine poem within sight of Gallipoli, inspired by thoughts of Achilles: 'I saw a man this morning who did not wish to die.'

There was no hint, in this group of friends, of their wanting a soft option. They certainly did not get it. The RND saw fierce front-line action at Suvla Bay. PSS came under fire for long periods, roughed it out in trenches and soldiered well. After some time he was switched to staff work, where he shone as liaison officer with the French. The

French made him a Chevalier of the Légion d'Honneur, and nominated him for a Croix de Guerre (Silver Star). After the Gallipoli campaign was abandoned he was posted to Salonica, served in Macedonia, and shone once more in the liaison role. But he began to fret for a move to the Western Front. Partly, one suspects, so as to be nearer home and nearer to the love of his life, Diana Manners (daughter of the Duke of Rutland). He felt (rightly) that she was slipping out of his reach into the clutches of Duff Cooper.

From the end of 1916, when he secured home leave, to the end of 1917, his story moved to a close. By early 1917 the RND was at Abbeville, then on the Somme, then up to Vimy Ridge. PSS rejoined for active service in May, his close friend Raymond Asquith in command of his unit. In October and November the Hood Battalion was in battle at Passchendaele, though PSS was behind the lines on special training. The battalion suffered heavy losses. Asquith was sent on leave (and later wounded). PSS, just promoted to Lieutenant-Commander (the RND still preserved naval ranks), took command and, after one last stressed interlude of home leave, returned to this command. Christmas was quiet. In a ferocious attack early on 30 December the Germans poured into the British trenches. PSS was first wounded and, fighting on, was quickly killed.

Diana Manners wrote movingly: 'His instantaneous death, and an end to his brave heart and his mind teeming with methodical designs for a life full of fine aims, fortune, and fulfilment. His memory will last as long as we who knew him live to remember.'

Deep love for him from a circle of close friends lay behind those words.

Richard Carden

2nd LIEUTENANT FREDERICK CORLEY

15 November 1887 – 12 April 1918

On 12 April 1918, the day after Field Marshal Haig's 'backs to the wall' Special Order of the Day, as part of the British resistance in Belgium to the final spring German offensive, 2nd Lieutenant Corley, along with others, was ordered to fill a breach in the defensive line in the Le Touquet sector. In what became known as the Battle of the Lys, after the river over which the 8th Battalion faced the Germans on the other side, Corley was one of the first casualties of what became three days of intensive fighting. The Border Regiment had taken responsibility for this area from 5 April. The following days had been relatively quiet but heavy shelling commenced on the morning of the 9th. In the afternoon, the back areas of the British forces were shelled with gas being used.

Heavy shelling continued in succeeding days with casualties mounting amongst the Border and other regiments holding the area. The front areas were shelled on the eve of the major battle but with little damage. After a brief lull, fighting intensified on the 11th and then on 12 April, the enemy, as the diaries of the Border Regiment record, 'pressed back our right flank and by means of a hurricane bombardment of our line of posts we were compelled to withdraw toward Neuve-Eglise, also known as Nieuwkerke.' Corley and one other were killed at Kortepyp and two others wounded. The fighting continued, though with less intensity, until the 25th and the Border Regiment were relieved on 30 April. The Germans then held the area until August when it was retaken by the 36th (Ulster) Division.

At the time of his death, Corley and his colleagues in the 8th Battalion had been serving in France and Belgium for two and a half years. A German officer of the Alpine Corps wrote after the war that, in the attack in which Corley had been killed, the Germans had gained 'only a few hundred metres of ground'. He went on to write: 'I think I must say that defenders on the British front in April 1918 were the best troops with whom we had crossed swords in the course of four and a quarter years.' Four months after Corley's death, the 8th Battalion was dissolved. Twenty-six officers had been lost in nearly three weeks of fighting.

By the time of his death, Frederick Charles Corley had served in the army for a total of 11 years, having first joined his native Royal Norfolk Regiment in September 1905. The second of the two sons of Charles Corley, a blacksmith and wheelwright, and Rebecca, he was born in Caston, Norfolk, a small village north-east of Thetford, three years after and 15 miles from the seat of Viscount Ipswich, also commemorated on The Travellers' War Memorial. With presumably little formal education, he was in service at St Chad's College (now Denstone College), Denstone, Staffordshire, between Stoke-on-Trent and Derby, by the time he was 13 years old.

Apparently life in service at an independent school provided little stimulation to an ambitious young man. Frederick wanted to see more of the world and he enlisted in the Royal Norfolk Regiment at age 18 years and nine months. By that time he had already acquired two distinctive tattoos: a palm leaf encircling a snake and cupid on his left arm and Lady Godiva on a horse in a wreath on his right. Perhaps as a consequence of a horse which had taken exception to his being shorn by Frederick's father, he had a scar on his buttock. Corley first served in South Africa and then Gibraltar before he was posted in 1911 with his regiment to Belgaum (now Belagavi) in Karnataka, in west central India. There, with the 2nd Battalion of the Norfolks, his occupation was recorded as 'clerk'.

On 16 December 1912, Corley left the Norfolks, joined the army reserves, and made his way to London and employment at The Travellers. Perhaps he felt an affinity with the club, having been a traveller himself. Having seen something of the world, he decided to return to his original civilian occupation, that of a waiter, but now in London. About 18 months after he started working at The Travellers, war broke out. Now 27 years old, and an experienced soldier, his talents were needed by a rapidly expanding British Army. He was mobilised on 16 August 1914 and posted again to the Royal Norfolk Regiment. Corley was later transferred to the Border Regiment as a Warrant Officer Class 2. On being called up from the reserves, he put down as his occupation 'butler', not waiter or clerk. The blacksmith's son had become a gentleman's gentleman.

After several promotions, the last being Company Quartermaster Sergeant of the Border Regiment, the army, short of officers, determined that Corley was of officer material. A headmaster, one J.H. Taylor, confirmed that he had achieved, one way or another, sufficient education to serve as an officer. He had been trained as an ambulance attendant while at Belgaum. A Major under whom he had served in the Norfolks wrote that he had been a 'reliable and satisfactory NCO' and that he would 'make a satisfactory officer'. There is no evidence to the contrary and he was commissioned on 24 December 1916. At that time, he was serving in the La Bassée Canal sector near Béthune. Corley was wounded twice, once having been shot in the head and back, once with injuries to his right knee, and each time returned to England for recuperation. During one of his terms of hospitalisation, he met a nurse, Margaret Morrison. They were married in Helensburgh, Dunbartonshire, at the end of February 1917. Their son, Frederick Charles, given the same names as his father, was born five weeks after his father was killed.

2nd Lieutenant Corley's service to his country is commemorated in several locations. On The Travellers' War Memorial the engraver mistook a 'C' for an 'E' so he is recorded as 'Lieutenant F.E. Corley'. He is listed on the war memorial of his native Caston and on Panel 6 of the Ploegsteert Memorial, Hainaut, Belgium.

Though Frederick Corley was only with the club for about a year and a half of his 30 years, his competence, ambition, loyalty, and valour demonstrated he was an indeed a gentleman among gentlemen, which is how we remember him.

Robert Taylor

LIEUTENANT VISCOUNT IPSWICH

24 July 1884 – 23 April 1918

Lieutenant Viscount Ipswich was one of the first casualties of the Royal Air Force, the Royal Flying Corps being merged on 1 April 1918 with the Royal Naval Air Service to form the RAF just 23 days before he died while in pilot training at Yatesbury aerodrome, near Calne, in Wiltshire. Born William Henry Alfred FitzRoy, he became known by the courtesy title Viscount Ipswich on the death of his uncle, Henry, Earl of Euston, son of the 7th Duke of Grafton in 1912. In civilian life, Lord Ipswich had worked as a surveyor in Wye, Kent, an occupation he had taken up some time after leaving Trinity College, Cambridge, which he had entered from Harrow in 1903.

Lord Ipswich started his military career not in the Royal Flying Corps, but in the 4th Buffs, the East Kent Regiment. Joining as a Private, he was transferred almost immediately to the recently created 4th Battalion of the Coldstream Guards, known as the Pioneers, and commissioned on 15 August 1914. His wife of just 11 months, Auriol, was then pregnant with their first child. Posted to the Western Front in France on 11 November 1914, he was invalided home on 20 May the following year. He was suffering from a cracked eardrum as a result of a shell explosion two days before. Unable to take the strain of combat, he was diagnosed the following year as suffering from 'neurasthenia', a now obsolete medical term for what was commonly known as shell shock. The symptoms include depression, extreme lassitude and an inability to deal with more than the simplest tasks. He was placed on leave and returned to his wife's family home, Potterspury House, Northamptonshire, to convalesce with his wife, their young son, and a daughter who was soon to be born.

Finally determined by a series of medical boards to be fit for light duties, Ipswich returned to service in August 1916. He was duly placed on light duties, doubtless desk work in England. Such work did not suit him and he somehow managed to get himself enrolled with the Royal Flying Corps initially, from October 1917, at Reading, and then, from the middle of December, at a course to train aerial observers at Winchester. He overcame his medical condition and started pilot training at Yatesbury training base, having undertaken a course on petrol engines and completed his observer training.

The first person to take Ipswich up in an aeroplane was Billy Cotton. Cotton, who subsequently became well-known on British television as a dance-band leader, was then a pilot trainer at Yatesbury. At their first meeting, Cotton remembered Ipswich to have been 'fresh-faced, full of enthusiasm, terribly polite'. Refusing Cotton's advice to change into more suitable clothing, Ipswich wore 'a lovely Burberry, GS tunic, and a smart shirt, which we never wore with our maternity jackets, immaculate puttees, the lot … He was most enthusiastic, but he was also very oily from the engine' after the flight. In those days, the pilot sat immediately behind a less than spotless petrol engine that spewed oil and fumes into the faces of the occupants of the aeroplane. When Ipswich returned to the mess, he is reported to have said: 'By God, wonderful, wonderful, wonderful', and was full of praise for Billy Cotton. When he and Cotton next met, Cotton once more advised him to dress down for flying behind the engine, but he merely remarked that he did not mind. Ipswich was 'a really good thoroughbred young man' in Cotton's opinion.

He soon passed his elementary pilot instruction and moved on to more advanced operational aeroplanes. However, Ipswich's flying career, which he pursued with the apparent zest that he had demonstrated as a bantam-weight boxer at Cambridge, soon ended tragically when he crashed his plane on 23 April 1918. He was flying a Royal Aircraft Factory R.E.8, an aeroplane with a reputation for being notoriously difficult to fly. Such planes, when used in training, were often reconstructed after earlier accidents. While at low altitude, he 'got into a vertical spin and crashed into the ground'. A Court of Inquiry ruled that he made 'an error of judgement turning [too] near the ground, causing the machine to stall'. Billy Cotton, who claims to have seen the accident, recalled many years later that he broke the back of the R.E.8 while doing a loop and 'came down without any wings'.

It fell to Lady Ipswich to come to Yatesbury to identify him. She arrived in the family Daimler, leaving in it their three year old son, John, now known as Viscount Ipswich who became the 9th Duke of Grafton in 1930. Lady Ipswich, who was pregnant at the time of his death, remarried in 1929 but died nine years later. Ipswich's son, John, perhaps with the same sense of adventure as his father, was killed on the first lap of the 1936 Limerick International Grand Prix. His Bugatti failed to negotiate an 'S' curve and burst into flames.

Lieutenant Viscount Ipswich was buried in St Genevieve's Churchyard, in the grounds of Euston Hall, the seat of the Dukes of Grafton, near Thetford, in Suffolk. He and another FitzRoy, Lieutenant

William Henry (1893–1917), who served in the Royal Navy and was on HMS *Simoom* when it was torpedoed in the North Sea, are commemorated in a war memorial just outside the gates of Euston Park. Lord Ipswich is also commemorated on the war memorial at Whittlebury, Northamptonshire, near his and his wife's home, Potterspury House, and Ascham Memorial Arch, Eastbourne, where he attended prep school.

Robert Taylor

BREVET MAJOR THE HONOURABLE GEORGE BOSCAWEN, DSO

6 December 1888 – 7 June 1918

George Boscawen was born on 6 December 1888, the second son of Major-General Evelyn, 7th Viscount Falmouth, whose first travels after election to the club in 1884 were on the expedition to relieve Gordon in Khartoum. The family's London home at 2 St James's Square was near the club. George attended Ludgrove and Eton before studying German in Freiburg. He joined the Royal Military Academy, Woolwich in January 1906.

At Woolwich, George became an Under Officer, won the Benson Memorial and Riding Prizes and represented the Academy at cricket, later playing at Combined Services level. Commissioned into the Royal Field Artillery in December 1907, George served in 119 Battery, XXVII Brigade RFA (artillery brigades then equate to regiments now) with its six 18-pounder field guns, initially at Deep Cut Huts, Frimley Green and, from late 1910, at Ballincollig, County Cork, the year in which he too joined The Travellers. Family tradition records that George was part of the British Observer Mission to the First Balkan War in 1912, although that December he journeyed to Canada to become aide-de-camp to HRH the Duke of Connaught, the Governor General.

After war broke out in 1914, George landed in France on 25 August. He joined 11 Battery, XV Brigade RFA on 19 September at Sainte-Marguerite, near Chivres on the river Aisne and was soon in action supporting Brigadier-General Count Gleichen's 15th Brigade (5th Division, II Corps). After 10 days fighting, the battery entrained for Festubert, near Béthune, and supported 15th Brigade's 'advance to contact'. The battery remained in action until the 30th with 15th Brigade on the rising ground around Festubert and Givenchy, north of the Aire-La Bassée canal. On 13 October, German infantry forced the 1st Battalion, Bedfordshire Regiment out of Givenchy: George's two guns held their positions until enemy troops were within 200 yards. They recovered the guns after dark. Promoted Captain on 30 October, George was awarded the Distinguished Service Order 'for gallantly fighting his section of guns in front of la Bassée … when all his detachment except himself was wounded and all infantry had fallen back from where his guns were'.

On 18 October, however, George became ADC to Lieutenant-General Sir Henry Rawlinson, commanding IV Corps, who had served with his father in the Coldstream Guards. George was present when George V visited Raymond Poincaré, President of France, and Generals Joffre and Foch, at Château Demont, Rawlinson's headquarters near Béthune on 1 December.

On 22 June 1915, George was mentioned in despatches, the first of five mentions. Shortly afterwards, he joined Headquarters IV Corps' Artillery staff, three weeks before the Battle of Loos. George remained on the artillery staff when Fourth Army formed under Rawlinson in 1916 before the Somme offensive. Gazetted Brevet Major on 3 June 1916, George became GSO II [artillery]. During his time on the Corps' and Army Artillery staffs, which spanned the Loos, Somme, and Arras offensives, George contributed not only to operational planning but also to transforming artillery into a highly technical, battle-winning force.

In September 1917, George left to gain regimental experience before commanding an artillery brigade. In February 1918, he took over 116 Siege Battery, with 6-inch 26-cwt 'heavy' howitzers, in LXXVII Brigade, Royal Garrison Artillery. The brigade fired at Passchendaele against the second German offensive in April before joining Lieutenant-General Sir Alexander Hamilton Gordon's IX Corps, comprising five British divisions which had suffered severely in the German offensive in March. The Corps took over a 'quiet' sector on the Chemin des Dames, above the river Aisne.

116 Siege Battery was beside the Anglo-French Corps boundary near Craonnelle when, on 26 May, intelligence warned of imminent attack. Colonel Bruchmüller orchestrated over 6,400 German guns, including some of the heaviest available, for Operation 'BLÜCHER' against the Chemin des Dames, and a three-hour bombardment – the heaviest of the war – opened at 1am on the 27th with high explosives, smoke and gas. The German infantry overran 50th (Northumbrian) Division during the assault.

116 Siege Battery had earlier fired successfully against enemy batteries, but when the barrage lifted, enemy troops were behind the battery position. The guns were blown up, and the battery made a stand with rifles. Two officers and eight other ranks were killed and an officer and 70 men were taken prisoner.

Around noon, Dr Kurt Schumann, veterinary surgeon to a German artillery regiment, found George seriously wounded near the 'very severely bombarded' battery position. Schumann arranged for him to be carried to a dressing station. George died of his wounds on 7 June in a German hospital at Notre-Dame de Liesse, near Laon. He is commemorated with a Special Memorial at La Ville-aux-Bois British Cemetery, three miles from the Aisne.

George Boscawen, a cricketer, accomplished horseman and game-shot, was a capable and courageous officer who had the potential, his contemporaries felt, to have reached high rank had he lived. His father, now Colonel of the Coldstream, knew when Western Front offensives were in the offing since the pheasants would not settle at night in Mereworth Woods, near Maidstone. After three years writing to parents and widows of Coldstreamers killed in action, he was devastated when George was reported missing, having lost another of his four sons, Vere, who was in the 1st Battalion Coldstream Guards, at Gheluvelt in October 1914. Major-General Boscawen died on 1 October 1918, aged 71.

Colonel Hugh Boscawen

LIEUTENANT WILLIAM LEVESON GOWER

12 March 1883 – 9 October 1918

William Leveson Gower was born in Rio de Janeiro, where his father was Third Secretary at the British Legation, and later spent time with him in several European capitals, including Athens. He travelled widely in Greece and elsewhere in the Balkans. He passed the Foreign Office exams in Modern Greek, as well as French and German, but did not join the Diplomatic Service, instead taking an appointment as a Clerk in the Journal Office of the House of Lords. He was called to the Bar at the Inner Temple in 1911.

Leveson Gower continued to take a close interest in Balkan affairs, especially Albania, which he visited in 1913, becoming a friend of Mehmet Bey Konitsa, later Albanian Foreign Minister and Ambassador in London, though they disagreed about the choice of Tirana as Albania's capital. He met Aubrey Herbert at The Travellers in February 1914 to discuss Albania. Other interests included support for the Working Men's College and lecturing for the Workers' Educational Association. Much of his spare time, however, was taken up with the Inns of Court Officer Training Corps, which he joined in 1907 as a Private, Mounted Infantry. He loved riding and had made himself an expert at shoeing horses. He was later commissioned as Lieutenant.

Leveson Gower seems to have taken on full-time duty with the OTC soon after the outbreak of war. In October 1915 he was seconded to the regular army and served as a staff officer in London and the Home Counties. In 1916 he was appointed temporary Captain. In December 1917 he returned to the OTC but was now keen to get to the front line. He may have been influenced by the example of his close friend, Robert Bailey, another Parliamentary Clerk, who was wounded in Palestine and died in Cairo on 1 December 1917. To this end he transferred to the Coldstream Guards in March 1918. Two of his first cousins were already serving with this regiment, and a third had been killed in action with it in August 1917.

After undergoing various training courses, Leveson Gower left for France on 10 September 1918, joining the 1st Battalion at the front on 30 September. Three days before his arrival, as part of a major allied offensive, the Guards Division had begun an assault against the Hindenburg Line, just west of Cambrai. 1 Coldstream had led the crossing of the heavily-defended Canal du Nord, suffering 151 casualties though winning two Victoria Crosses. Leveson Gower joined the battalion in the trenches behind the front where they were resting near Boursies on the main road from Cambrai to Bapaume. He wrote bright, cheerful letters home. On 2 October, he described his situation as: 'quite snug and comfortable; bath water's a bit scarce but what does that matter when you are in the perfect battalion? And it really is. I was never in such an officers' mess and the men are more than all one could wish them to be, and haven't we got our tails up!'

Over the following days the advance continued to the east and north-east and on 8 October 2nd Guards Brigade, including 1 Coldstream, reached Forenville, south-east of Cambrai. The next morning when the general advance resumed at 5.20am, 1 Coldstream were on the extreme left of the line. Although Leveson Gower had only been with the battalion for a week, he was in charge of No 3 Company, which was initially held in reserve. In a letter home on 7 October he described this command of a Company of the Coldstream as 'an ambition beyond my wildest dreams'. In the darkness, in intense cold, and under a British barrage, the battalion worked their way forward, taking their first objective, the La Targette-Cambrai road, and then pushing on to the railway. While the leading companies crossed the Cambrai-Le Cateau road and dug in beyond it, No 3 Company remained for a time on the railway and Leveson Gower with his orderly walked a short way up the railway in order to get in touch with the West Kent Regiment, who were on the Coldstream's left but not up to the line. At about 10am, while he was talking to an officer of the West Kent Regiment, a shell landed almost on top of them. Leveson Gower, gravely wounded in several places, was reported to have died instantaneously. The West Kent officer and several men were also killed. A West Kent orderly was sent off to inform the Coldstream and Lieutenant Victor Goodman, the battalion Intelligence Officer, immediately went down to identify the body, collect his personal belongings and make a sketch map of the location. Goodman, who wrote to Leveson Gower's father about the circumstances of his death, survived the war, winning an MC, and became Clerk of the Parliaments.

The Battle of Cambrai was to be the Coldstream Guards' last major battle honour of the war. The town itself was taken by Canadian forces on 9 October, the day of Leveson Gower's death, and the advance continued, with final success achieved on 7 November with the liberation of Maubeuge.

Leveson Gower was buried by the West Kent Regiment near where he fell, but after the war the grave was moved to the Awoingt British Cemetery. A memorial service was held at St George's Chapel, Windsor. His name is included in the House of Lords' war memorial in the Royal Gallery and, with his friend, Robert Bailey's, in a plaque in Eton College Chapel.

A family friend wrote in a tribute in *The Times*:

> 'His friends will remember him for many gifts – the gift of youth, of slow growth and steady ripening of powers, the gift of friendship, a rare delicacy of scruple, and sterling courage. Brave, affectionate, soldierly, he drew to himself the trust and the admiration of those who knew him. In the Army for which nature had fitted him, and for which he had long trained himself, he found a new metier. He loved his men, and they him. He was the friend of many children.'

A fellow Company Commander said that he 'greatly admired the way he, who had so little experience of conditions in France, took over command and ran so successfully a company which he had so little chance of getting to know.' Other tributes noted his reserve, modesty and generosity as a friend. In his will he left 20 remembrances to godchildren and other children.

One of Leveson Gower's sisters cherished her brother's papers and left them, with photographs and other items, to the Parliamentary Archive. All his sisters and brother, like him, died unmarried.

Nigel Cox

Index

Names of the Fifty are given in **bold** type.